crochet dolls
inspired by nature

crochet dolls
inspired by nature

20 amigurumi toys
celebrating the beauty
of biodiversity

Nathalie Amiel

DAVID & CHARLES
—PUBLISHING—

www.davidandcharles.com

Contents

General techniques

Introduction

Welcome to a journey into the heart of nature, where every loop brings to life the beauty and wonder of our natural world. In this book, we'll celebrate not just the importance of nature, but the pure joy it brings. From majestic oceans to serene lakes, and vibrant forests to windswept deserts, nature is a tapestry of life, woven with love, resilience, and interconnectedness.

This book is a testament to my profound passion and respect for the environment, captured in the form of unique crochet dolls. Each figure represents a different part of the incredible biodiversity of our planet. Together, they tell the story of nature's grandeur and its delicate balance using the special art of crochet.

Through these dolls, I hope to share how every part of nature plays a vital role in keeping our world balanced. From vast oceans and forests to small-but-mighty leaves and insects, they all work together in the beautiful dance of life. These elements not only support our ecosystems but also provide us with endless wonder and delight.

Of course, this book is not just about admiring nature – it's also about enjoying the precious craft of crochet. In it, you'll find a great variety of techniques and tips to enhance your crochet skills. Using basic stitches and more advanced techniques, each doll is designed to be both fun and inspiring. Whether you are a beginner or an experienced crocheter, there's something here for you to enjoy.

So, pick up your hooks and yarn and join me in this celebration of nature's wonders. Let's crochet a world where every doll tells a story of love, awareness, and the marvel of biodiversity. Enjoy the journey, and may these creations bring as much joy to you as nature does to all of us.

How to use this book

While all of the dolls in this book look unique, they each start with a common pattern (see Making the basic doll) before being completed with individual details.

The patterns generally use the amigurumi method of working in a spiral without joining each round with a slip stitch, unless otherwise stated. It will help to use a stitch marker in the first stitch of each round, so you know when you have completed the round. Move the marker up as you work.

Sizing

You can use any yarn and matching hook size to create your dolls. Note that, if you change the yarn weight and hook size up or down, your finished doll will be larger or smaller than the size given in the instructions for the project.

All patterns include the size for the doll, as well as their companion.

Gauge/tension

Using the hook and yarn mentioned in the pattern, 3 sc stitches and 4 Rounds/Rows measure 1 x 1cm (approx ½in x ½in).

IMPORTANT: If your tension is different, you might have to adjust your stitches when connecting the legs and the arms to the body.

Abbreviations

BLO: back loop only

ch: chain

ch sp(s): chain space(s)

cm: centimetre

dc: double crochet

dc-cl: double crochet cluster

FLO: front loop only

g: gram

hdc: half double crochet

in: inch

invdec: invisible decrease

m: metre

mm: millimetre

oz: ounce

p: picot

rs: right side

sc: single crochet

sc2tog: single crochet 2 stitches together

sc3tog: single crochet 3 stitches together

slst: slip stitch

st(s): stitch(es)

trbl: treble

tr-cl: treble cluster

yds: yards

[ ]: work instructions within brackets as many times as directed

*: repeat instructions following the asterisk as directed

See General techniques section for stitch instructions.

US/UK terminology

All the patterns in this book are written using US crochet terms. See the table below for the equivalent UK stitch names.

US term	UK term
single crochet	double crochet
double crochet	treble crochet
half double crochet	half treble crochet
treble	double treble
yarn over hook	yarn round hook
skip	miss

Useful tips

- Read all of the instructions carefully before you start working on your dolls.

- Go slowly and carefully while stuffing your dolls, making sure you use small amounts of stuffing at a time and shaping your doll as you work.

- Make sure you crochet your chains very loosely, it will be much easier to work into them later.

- When (re)connecting your yarn to your work, start with a loop on your hook so you can create the first stitch right away (it will make the connected stitch look much neater).

- When changing colours, switch to the new colour when pulling the yarn through the loops of the previous colour.

- Make sure to use a small size hook to avoid having gaps in your work.

- If you're making a doll for a small child, you can embroider the eyes rather than using safety eyes.

Tools and materials

Here, you'll find a list of everything necessary to make your precious dolls. Hooks and yarns are the most important things, but there are some other materials you'll need for adding those little details and creating the most beautiful dolls.

Crochet hooks

You will need crochet hooks in the following sizes to make the items in this book: 2mm, 2.25mm, and 2.5mm. The US equivalent for all these sizes is US B/1, so we have not added this conversion to each project individually.

Yarn

These are the yarns I've used, but you can choose any yarn to make your dolls unique and special.

- Scheepjes Organicon; 100% organic cotton; 50g (1¾oz)/170m (186yds); 4-ply (fingering weight).

- Krea Deluxe Organic Cotton; 100% organic cotton; 50g (1¾oz)/165m (180yds); 4-ply (fingering weight).

- TeDdY's Wool Starlight Silver; 50% rayon, 41% metallic, 9% nylon; 50g (1¾oz)/137m (150yds); lace weight.

- Black and white embroidery yarn (floss).

- Glow-in-the-dark embroidery yarn.

Most of the patterns in this book use yarn scraps. If more is needed (for example for the hair or dress) the yarn amount will be stated at the beginning of the pattern.

Other tools and materials

- **Stuffing**
  Any toy stuffing of your choice.

- **Wire**
  0.5mm (24 gauge) thickness wire for the doll frame.

- **Jewellery pliers**
  For shaping the wire frame.

- **Eyes**
  7mm, 6mm, 4mm safety eyes or black embroidery yarn.

- Tapestry needle.

- Stitch markers.

- **Blush**
  For cheeks and ears.

- **Acrylic paint**
  For freckles.

- **Strong cardboard or plastic**
  For shoes.

- **Small pet brush**
  For fluffing yarn.

Making the basic doll

All of the projects in this book use a basic pattern for the dolls' arms, heads and torsos. This makes things simple if you plan to make lots of dolls, as you will soon get the hang of crocheting the various parts.

Start by choosing the doll you would like to create. The instructions for each project tell you whether to follow the Large Doll pattern or the Small Doll pattern for the arms, head and torso.

First, make the arms and head following the general pattern instructions given on the following pages. Then follow the pattern for your specific doll to create the legs or tail. Return to the general instructions for the torso, neck and hair. Finally, head back to the doll of your choice for the finishing touches and special details. All of the basic and specific patterns use standard abbreviations – these are explained on the How to use this book pages.

The General Techniques section is on hand to help you master the skills you need to make the dolls. It includes a stitch gallery, along with instructions on making a magic ring, increasing and decreasing, and assembling your doll. The Templates section includes wire-frame templates and handy tips on making and inserting the frames.

Basic doll

Arms for both sizes (make 2)

Using 2.25mm hook and the yarn colour of your choice, ch 3.

Round 1: Skip last st of ch, 1 sc into one side of ch, 3 sc into first st of ch, 1 sc into opposite side of ch. (5 sts)

Place marker.

Round 2: 3 sc into first st, 1 sc, 3 sc into next st, 2 sc. (9 sts)

Rounds 3 and 4: 9 sc.

Round 5: Invdec, 2 sc, invdec, 3 sc. (7 sts)

Rounds 6 to 17: 7 sc.

(A)- Fasten off and set aside.

Large head

Using 2.25mm hook and the yarn colour of your choice, make a magic ring.

Round 1: 6 sc into ring. (6 sts)

Round 2: [2 sc in next st] 6 times. (12 sts)

Round 3: [2 sc in next st, 1 sc] 6 times. (18 sts)

Round 4: [2 sc in next st, 2 sc] 6 times. (24 sts)

Round 5: [2 sc in next st, 3 sc] 6 times. (30 sts)

Round 6: [2 sc in next st, 4 sc] 6 times. (36 sts)

Round 7: [2 sc in next st, 5 sc] 6 times. (42 sts)

Rounds 8 to 13: 42 sc.

(B)- Use a piece of yarn scrap to mark where the eyes will be placed, between Rounds 13 and 14, one between sts 17 and 18, the other between sts 24 and 25 (there are 7 sts between the eyes).

Round 14: 14 sc, [2 sc in next st, 1 sc] 2 times, [2 sc in next st] 6 times, [1 sc, 2 sc in next st] 2 times, 14 sc. (52 sts)

Rounds 15 to 20: 52 sc.

Insert 7mm eyes.

Round 21: [Invdec] 26 times. (26 sts)

Stuff the head firmly.

Round 22: [3 sc, invdec] 5 times, 1 sc. (21 sts)

(C)- Stuff the head some more, taking care to fill out the forehead and cheeks nicely.

Round 23: [invdec, 1 sc] 7 times. (14 sts)

Round 24: [invdec] 7 times. (7 sts)

(D)- Fasten off and leave a long tail.

Nose

(E)- Embroider a little nose over 2 sts between Rounds 12 and 13, between the eyes.

Small head

Using 2.25mm hook and the yarn colour of your choice, make a magic ring.

Round 1: 6 sc into ring. (6 sts)

Round 2: [2 sc in next st] 6 times. (12 sts)

Round 3: [2 sc in next st, 1 sc] 6 times. (18 sts)

Round 4: [2 sc in next st, 2 sc] 6 times. (24 sts)

Round 5: [2 sc in next st, 3 sc] 6 times. (30 sts)

Round 6: [2 sc in next st, 4 sc] 6 times. (36 sts)

Round 7: [2 sc in next st, 17 sc] 2 times. (38 sts)

Rounds 8 to 12: 38 sc.

(B)- Use a piece of yarn scrap to mark where the eyes will be placed, between Rounds 12 and 13, one between sts 15 and 16, the other between sts 22 and 23 (there are 7 sts between the eyes).

Round 13: 14 sc, 2 sc in next st, 1 sc, [2 sc in next st] 6 times, 1 sc, 2 sc in next st, 14 sc. (46 sts)

Rounds 14 to 18: 46 sc.

Insert 6mm eyes.

Round 19: [Invdec] 22 times. (23 sts)

Stuff the head firmly.

Round 20: Invdec, 21 sc. (22 sts)

(C)- Stuff the head some more, taking care to fill out the forehead and cheeks nicely.

Round 21: [Invdec] 11 times. (11 sts)

Round 22: [Invdec, 2 sc] 2 times, invdec. (8 sts)

Round 23: Invdec (stop Round here) (7 sts)

(D)- Fasten off and leave a long tail.

Nose

Embroider a little nose over 2 sts between Rounds 12 and 13, between the eyes.

Embroidering the eyes

E – With white embroidery yarn, make a horizontal stitch from sts 16 to 17 and from sts 24 to 25. Keep the stitches loose. Do the same with black embroidery yarn.

The safety eyes will partially cover the embroidered lines.

Make sure you check the pattern for the specific doll you are creating – embroidery of additional lashes may be needed!

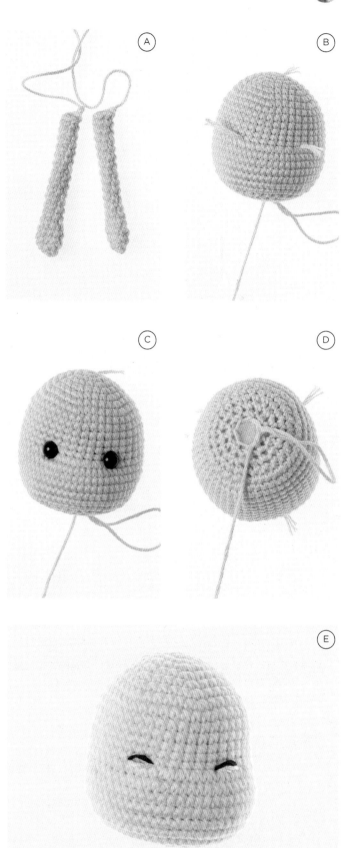

Large doll torso and neck

After creating the legs of your doll (according to its specific pattern), continue working in the round.

Round 1: [6 sc, invdec] 4 times. (28 sts)

Rounds 2 to 6: 28 sc.

Round 7: 7 sc, 7 sc around first arm, 14 sc of body, 7 sc around second arm, 7 sc. (42 sts)

Round 8: 6 sc, invdec, 6 sc, invdec, 10 sc, invdec, 6 sc, invdec, 6 sc. (38 sts)

Round 9: 4 sc, invdec, 6 sc, invdec, 9 sc, invdec, 6 sc, invdec, 5 sc. (34 sts)

Stuff just the tips of the hands, insert your wire frame (see Templates) and press stuffing into the tummy and back.

Round 10: 3 sc, invdec, 6 sc, invdec, 8 sc, invdec, 6 sc, invdec, 3 sc. (30 sts)

Stuff the shoulders nicely.

Round 11: [3 sc, invdec] 6 times. (24 sts)

Round 12: [2 sc, invdec] 6 times. (18 sts)

Round 13: [1 sc, invdec] 6 times. (12 sts)

Round 14: [1 sc, invdec] 4 times. (8 sts)

Round 15: invdec, 6 sc. (7 sts)

Round 16: 7 sc.

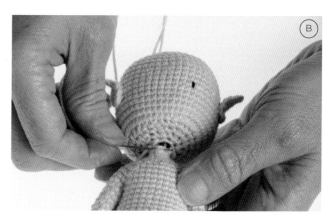

Place the head onto the neck and use small even stitches to sew on tightly.

Fasten off, close all gaps and weave in ends.

Small doll torso and neck

After creating the legs of your doll (according to its specific pattern), continue working in the round.

Round 1: [5 sc, invdec] 4 times. (24 sts)

Rounds 2 to 5: 24 sc.

Round 6: 6 sc, 7 sc around first arm, 12 sc of body, 7 sc around second arm, 6 sc. (38 sts)

Round 7: 5 sc, invdec, 6 sc, invdec, 9 sc, invdec, 6 sc, invdec, 4 sc. (34 sts)

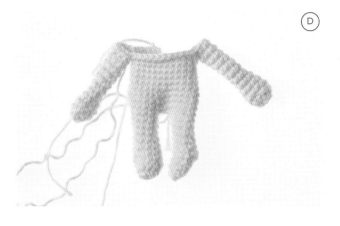

Round 8: 5 sc, invdec, 4 sc, invdec, 8 sc, invdec, 4 sc, invdec, 5 sc. (30 sts)

Stuff just the tips of the hands, insert your wire frame (see Templates) and press stuffing into the tummy and back.

Round 9: [1 sc, invdec] 10 times. (20 sts)

Stuff the shoulders nicely.

Round 10: [2 sc, invdec] 5 times. (15 sts)

Round 11: [invdec] 7 times, 1 sc. (8 sts)

Round 12: invdec, 6 sc. (7 sts)

Round 13: 7 sc.

Place the head onto the neck and use small even stitches to sew on tightly.

Fasten off, close all gaps and weave in ends.

Hair

The best way ever to crochet hair!

(A) Mark the hairline all the way round the head with
(B) a piece of embroidery yarn.

Measure out a piece of yarn double the length
you want the hair to be and fold it in half
creating a loop. Do not cut the yarn.

(C) Insert your crochet hook into any of the stitches
(D) along the hairline and pull up the loop.

(E) Wrap the shorter piece of yarn around your hook
from front to back.

(F) yo the long end of the yarn and pull through
(G) both loops on your hook. Continue this way until
your hair strand has the desired length. Then
wrap both yarns around your hook and pull
through the loop. Cut the yarn short and tighten.

Repeat this all around the hairline and the entire
head. Create strands on every second round and
into every second stitch (so there won't be too
much hair).

A

B

C

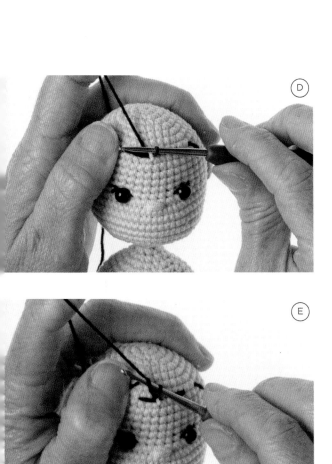

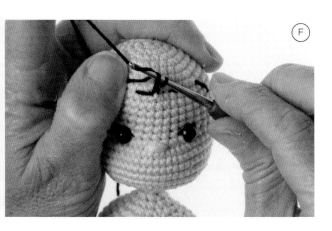

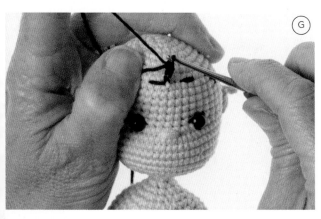

The dolls

Meet the Crochet Dolls Inspired by Nature – each one representing a unique and vital part of our world.

The Ocean King rules the deep, powerful seas, while the Sun Queen shines her warmth over everything that grows. As the Flower Princess conjures beauty and blooms, the Bird Fairy fills the skies with her vibrant energy. The Arctic Prince reigns over frozen lands, while the Insect Lord keeps the small but mighty bugs buzzing in harmony. Tranquil waters are the realm of the Lady of the Lake, the Mushroom Sprite nurtures the hidden wonders beneath the forest floor and the Night Nymph guards the mysteries of twilight. The Tree Prince stretches his arms to connect the earth and sky.

Together, these precious dolls make up a colourful cast of characters, each playing their part in nature's incredible story. They remind us that every corner of the natural world is filled with wonder and that even the smallest creatures and quietest places have their own roles to fulfil. Let them take you on an unforgettable crochet adventure through forests, lakes, skies, and seas, where magic is always around the corner and nature's beauty never stops inspiring!

Bird Fairy
& Hummingbird

The Bird Fairy reigns over the skies, where winged wonders soar through the air with beauty and grace. She ensures the well-being and vitality of bird populations, from majestic eagles to delicate hummingbirds and melodious songbirds. As the protector of avian enchantment, the Bird Fairy plays a crucial role in maintaining the balance and harmony of the bird world.

Birds are essential components of global ecosystems, contributing to pollination, seed dispersal, and insect control. They also serve as indicators of environmental health, signalling changes in habitat quality and ecosystem stability. Additionally, birds inspire wonder and admiration through their stunning plumage, intricate songs, and remarkable migratory journeys.

The Bird Fairy symbolises the beauty and importance of birds in our natural world. By honouring and preserving her realm, we celebrate the diversity of birdlife and safeguard their habitats for future generations to marvel at and cherish.

DIFFICULTY LEVEL: INTERMEDIATE

Bird Fairy

Finished size: 14cm (5½in)

YARNS

Krea Deluxe Organic Cotton 29, Scheepjes Organicon Perfect Plum (257), Scheepjes Organicon Lucky Heather (259), Scheepjes Organicon Lavender Haze (204), Scheepjes Organicon Lavender (205), Scheepjes Organicon Dahlia (246), Teddy's Wool Starlight Silver

HOOKS

2.25mm, 2.5mm

Arms and head

Use 2.25mm hook and Krea Deluxe Organic Cotton 29.

Make the arms using the general pattern instructions (see Making the basic doll) and stop after Round 11.

Make the head following the small head instructions (see Making the basic doll).

Lashes

Embroider 2 small lashes on the outside of the eyes.

Feet and legs

Using 2.25mm hook and Krea Deluxe Organic Cotton 29, ch 3.

Round 1: Skip last st of ch, 1 sc into one side of ch, 3 sc into first st of ch, 1 sc into opposite side of ch. (5 sts)

Place marker.

Round 2: 3 sc into first st, 1 sc, 3 sc in next st, 2 sc. (9 sts)

Round 3: 9 sc.

Create the heel by working back and forth, do not ch 1 after turn.

(A) **Row 4:** 5 sc, turn, sc2tog, 1 sc, sc2tog.

Continue working in the round.

Round 5: Turn, 3 sc, 1 sc into space between heel and top of foot, 5 sc into top of foot, 1 sc into space between top of foot and heel. (10 sts)

Place marker.

Round 6: 3 sc, invdec, 3 sc, invdec. (8 sts)

Rounds 7 to 10: 8 sc.

Round 11: [2 sc in next st, 3 sc] 2 times. (10 sts)

Rounds 12 to 17: 10 sc.

(B) **Round 18:** 4 sc.

Fasten off and set aside to attach to second leg later. Make second leg the same through to Round 17, then work 8 sc to move to joining point.

Round 18: Ch 2, connect by 10 sc around first leg, starting after the fastened-off st, 2 sc into ch, 10 sc around second leg, 2 sc into opposite side of ch. (24 sts)

NOTE: Adjust sts if necessary to make sure both feet are facing forward by sc more or fewer sts around the legs in Round 18.

Place marker.

Body

(C) Continue working in the round for body.

Round 1: [1 sc, 2 sc in next st] 2 times, 14 sc, [2 sc in next st, 1 sc] 2 times, 2 sc. (28 sts)

Rounds 2 to 4: 28 sc.

Stuff the tips of the toes, insert your wire frame and continue stuffing the legs.

Work torso and neck according to general pattern instructions (see Making the basic doll).

D - Hair

Yarn quantity: 50g (1¾oz)

Using 2.25mm hook and Scheepjes Organicon Lavender Haze (204), measure out about 100cm (39in) and create the hair following the general instructions (see Making the basic doll), making hair strands 35 to 45 sts long.

Dress

The first part of the dress is made working back and forth. Turn and ch after each row (ch is not counted as st).

Using 2.5mm hook and Scheepjes Organicon Lavender (205), ch 26.

Row 1: Skip last st of ch, [4 sc, 2 sc in next st] 5 times. (30 sts). Turn, ch 1.

Row 2: BLO [5 sc, 2 sc in next st] 5 times. (35 sts)

E - **Row 3:** 2 sc in next st, 2 sc, 2 sc in next st, ch 2, skip next 8 sts, 2 sc in next st, 3 sc, [2 sc in next st] 3 times, 3 sc, 2 sc in next st, ch 2, skip next 8 sts, 2 sc in next st, 2 sc, 2 sc in next st. (28 sts + 4 ch)

Row 4: 2 sc in next st, 4 sc, 2 sc in next st, 2 sc in ch, 16 sc, 2 sc in ch, 2 sc in next st, 4 sc, 2 sc in next st. (36 sts)

Switch to Scheepjes Organicon Lucky Heather (259).

Close to form a circle by dc into first sts in the next round. Continue working in the round.

F - **Round 5:** FLO [2 dc in next st] 36 times. (72 sts)

Round 6: [2 hdc in next st, 1 hdc] 36 times. (108 sts)

Rounds 7 to 9: 108 hdc.

Switch to Teddy's Wool Starlight Silver.

Round 10: BLO [skip next st, 5 hdc in next st, skip next st, slst in next st] 25 times. Fasten off and weave in ends.

Underskirt

(A) Using 2.5mm hook and Scheepjes Organicon Perfect Plum (257), connect your yarn to the first BLO of Round 5.

Round 1: BLO [2 dc in next st] 36 times. (72 sts)

Rounds 2 to 5: 72 dc.

Switch to Scheepjes Organicon Dahlia (246).

(B) **Round 6:** [3 dc in next st] 72 times. (216 sts)

(C) Fasten off and weave in ends.

Wings

Short feathers

Use 2.25mm hook and Scheepjes Organicon Perfect Plum (257).

(D) Ch 14, skip last sts of ch and pull up 13 loops working into each st of ch. * Keep the first and last loop short but make the other loops about 3mm (⅛in) long. You have 14 loops waiting on your hook.

(E) **Row 1:** [Yarn over and pull through 2 loops on your hook] 13 times, you have just one loop left on your hook **, make a p, turn.

(F) Start pulling up loops from the FLO of ch. Repeat from * until **, 14 slst into each st on the top of the feather, slst back into very first ch st.

(G) Fasten off, leave long yarn tail to sew the feathers to each other later.

Make two feathers in each of the two colours: Scheepjes Organicon Perfect Plum (257) and Scheepjes Organicon Lucky Heather (259).

Medium feathers

Ch 16 and create the feathers using the same technique as for the short feather. Pull up 15 loops. Make two feathers in each of the two colours: Scheepjes Organicon Lavender (205) and Scheepjes Organicon Dahlia (246).

Large feathers

Ch 18 and create the feathers using the same technique as for the short feather.

Make two feathers in each of the two colours: Scheepjes Organicon Lucky Heather (259) and Scheepjes Organicon Lavender (205).

(H)
(I) Arrange the 12 feathers according to size and colour on top of each other in a fan shape and sew them together tightly. Sew the feather fan onto the right back opening of the dress tightly. Repeat for the left side.

(J) Put the dress on the doll and close the back opening.

Flowers

Using 2.25mm hook and Teddy's Wool Starlight Silver, make a magic ring.

Small flower

Round 1: [ch 1, 2 hdc, ch 1, slst into ring] 5 times. Fasten off and leave a long tail for sewing.

Large flower

Round 1: 10 sc into ring. (10 sts)

Switch to Scheepjes Organicon Dahlia (246).

Round 2: [ch 1, 2 hdc, ch 1, slst into previous st] 5 times. Fasten off and leave a long tail for sewing.

Sew the large flower in between the wings and the small flower to the front of the dress.

Hair decorations

Create a few flowers and a few more feathers in different colours and sizes. Put the hair up in two buns and decorate it by sewing in the flowers and feathers.

Tie a piece of Teddy's Wool Starlight Silver around the doll's forehead for her crown.

Little Hummingbird Friend

Finished size: 6.5cm (2½in)

YARNS

Scheepjes Organicon Perfect Plum (257), Scheepjes Organicon Dahlia (246), Scheepjes Organicon Lucky Heather (259), Scheepjes Organicon Sapling (213), Scheepjes Organicon Deep Azure (263)

HOOK

2.25mm

Head and body

Make 3 mini pompoms (about 5cm (2 in) in circumference).

Pompom 1: use Scheepjes Organicon Deep Azure (263), Scheepjes Organicon Perfect Plum (257), Scheepjes Organicon Dahlia (246).

Pompom 2: use Scheepjes Organicon Lucky Heather (259), Scheepjes Organicon Sapling (213), Scheepjes Organicon Deep Azure (263).

Pompom 3: use Scheepjes Organicon Lucky Heather (259), Scheepjes Organicon Perfect Plum (257), Scheepjes Organicon Dahlia (246).

(A) Thread the 3 pompoms together to form the head and body of the Hummingbird and trim with scissors until you get a small bird shape.

Beak

Using 2.25mm hook and Scheepjes Organicon Perfect Plum (259), ch 6.

(B) **Row 1:** Skip last st of ch, 5 sc into ch. (5 sts)

Fasten off and leave a long tail to sew onto the bird's head tightly.

Wings and tail feathers

Make 2 feathers in each of the following colours: Scheepjes Organicon Dahlia (246), Scheepjes Organicon Perfect Plum (257) and Scheepjes Organicon Dahlia (246).

(C)
(D) Using 2.25mm hook, ch 10, skip last sts of ch and pull up 9 loops from each st of ch. Keep the first and last loops short but make the other loops about about 6mm (¼in) long. You have 10 loops waiting on your hook.

Row 1: [Yarn over and pull through 2 loops on your hook] 9 times, you have just one loop left on your hook, p, turn.

(E) **Row 2:** [1 slst, 9 sc] into FLO of ch.

(F) Fasten off, leave long yarn tail to sew the feathers to each other later.

(G) Make 3 feathers for each wing, sew them together to form a fan shape and sew to each side of the body tightly.

For the tail, make 5 feathers in total using the following colours: Scheepjes Organicon Perfect Plum (257), Scheepjes Organicon Dahlia (246) and Scheepjes Organicon Sapling (213). Sew them together to form a fan shape and stitch tightly to the back of the bird.

(H) Eyes

Glue 4mm safety eyes on each side of the beak. If you're making the bird for a small child, embroider the eyes instead.

Did you know?

Hummingbirds are incredible creatures known for their agility and speed! They can flap their wings up to 80 times per second, allowing them to hover and even fly backwards. Despite their small size, hummingbirds have high metabolisms and need to consume nectar frequently. They play a vital role in ecosystems by pollinating flowers, which is essential for plant reproduction and biodiversity. These birds also migrate long distances each year, showcasing their remarkable endurance and adaptability.

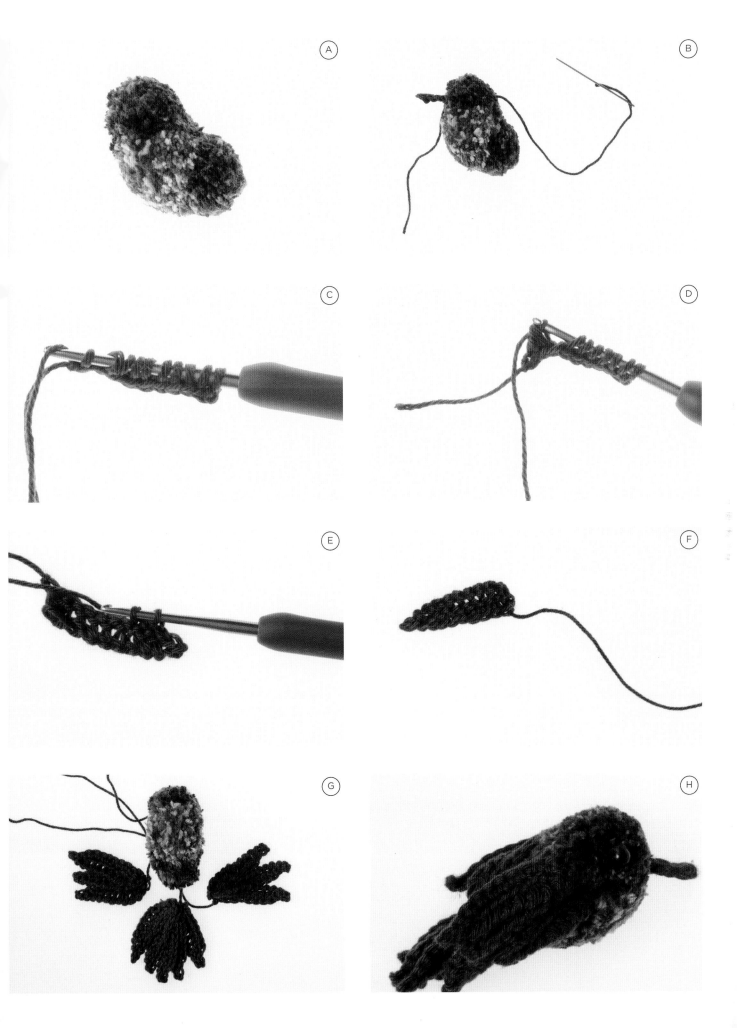

Flower Princess & Bee

The Flower Princess floats gracefully among blossoms, bringing enchantment to meadows and gardens. She ensures the health and balance of floral ecosystems, from delicate wildflowers to majestic blooms and intricate pollination networks.

Flowers are not mere ornaments; they are vital to ecosystems worldwide, providing food and shelter for insects, birds, and other wildlife. They play a crucial role in pollination, ensuring the reproduction of countless plant species and supporting global food production.

The Flower Princess embodies the deep connection between plants and the natural world. By honouring her, we honour the importance of flowers in ecological processes, biodiversity conservation, and human joy. Let us cherish the magnificence of floral diversity, striving to protect habitats and the significance of flowers in our natural world.

DIFFICULTY LEVEL: EASY TO INTERMEDIATE

Flower Princess

Finished size: 18cm (7in)

YARNS

Scheepjes Organicon Powder Pink (250),
Scheepjes Organicon Pink Petunia (249),
Scheepjes Organicon Pink Elephant (248),
Scheepjes Organicon Apple Blossom (207),
Scheepjes Organicon Soft Blossom (206),
Teddy's Wool Starlight Silver

HOOKS

2.25mm, 2.5mm

Arms and head

(A) Using 2.25mm hook and Scheepjes Organicon Powder Pink (250), make the arms and head following the general pattern instructions for the Large Doll (see Making the basic doll)

Lashes

Embroider 2 small lashes on the outside of the eyes.

Then make the legs and lower body following the instructions below:

Feet and legs

Using 2.25mm hook and Scheepjes Organicon Powder Pink (250), ch 4.

Round 1: Skip last st of ch, 2 sc into one side of ch, 3 sc into first st of ch, 2 sc into opposite side of ch. (7 sts)

Place marker.

Round 2: 3 sc into first st, 2 sc, 3 sc in next st, 3 sc. (11 sts)

Round 3: 11 sc.

Create the heel by working back and forth, do not ch 1 after turn.

Row 4: 7 sc, turn, sc2tog, 2 sc, sc2tog. Turn.

Continue working in the round.

Round 5: 4 sc, 1 sc into space between heel and top of foot, 6 sc into top of foot, 1 sc into space between top of foot and heel. (12 sts)

Place marker.

Round 6: 4 sc, invdec, 4 sc, invdec. (10 sts)

Rounds 7 to 9: 10 sc.

Round 10: [2 sc in next st, 4 sc] 2 times. (12 sts)

Round 11: [2 sc in next st, 5 sc] 2 times. (14 sts)

Rounds 12 to 15: 14 sc.

Round 16: [6 sc, 2 sc in next st] 2 times. (16 sts)

Round 17: [3 sc, 2 sc in next st] 4 times. (20 sts)

Rounds 18 to 27: 20 sc.

Round 28: 6 sc. Stop here.

Fasten off and set aside to attach to second leg later. Make second leg the same through to Round 27, then work 16 sc to move to joining point.

(B) **Round 28:** Ch 2, connect by 20 sc around first leg, starting after the fastened-off st, 2 sc into ch, 20 sc around second leg, 2 sc into opposite side of ch. (44 sts)

NOTE: Adjust sts if necessary to make sure both feet are facing forward by sc more or fewer sts around the legs in Round 28.

Place marker.

Body

Continue working in the round for body.

Round 1: [2 sc, 2 sc in next st] 3 times, 22 sc, [2 sc in next st, 2 sc] 3 times, 4 sc. (50 sts)

Rounds 2 to 7: 50 sc.

Stuff the tips of the toes, insert your wire frame, continue stuffing the legs.

Round 8: [3 sc, invdec] 10 times. (40 sts)

Round 9: 40 sc.

Round 10: [3 sc, invdec] 8 times. (32 sts)

Work torso and neck using general pattern instructions (see Making the basic doll).

(C) Hair

Yarn quantity: 50g (1¾oz)

Using Scheepjes Organicon Soft Blossom (206), measure about 100cm (39in) and create the hair following the general instructions (see Making the basic doll), making hair strands 35 to 45 sts long.

To make the curly ends:

After you make your chain, don't cut the yarn and continue working with the long strand; ch 1, [2 sc into next st of ch, 3 sc] 3 times, slst to fasten off. Weave in end.

Dress

 Top

The top of the dress is worked back and forth. Turn and ch at the end of each row (this ch does not count as a st).

Using 2.5mm hook and Scheepjes Organicon Pink Petunia (249), ch 34.

Row 1: Skip first st of ch, [10 sc, 2 sc into next st] 3 times. (36 sts). Turn, ch 1.

Row 2: FLO [5 sc, 2 sc in next st] 6 times. (42 sts). Turn, ch 1.

Row 3: 2 sc in first st, 5 sc, 2 sc in next st, 2 ch, skip 7 sts, 2 sc in next st, 5 sc, [2 sc in next st] 2 times, 5 sc, 2 sc in next sts, 2 ch, skip 7 sts, 2 sc in next st, 5 sc, 2 sc in next st. (36 sts + 4 ch). Turn, ch 1.

Row 4: 9 sc, 2 sc in ch, 18 sc, 2 sc in ch, 9 sc. (40 sts)

Rows 5 to 8: 40 sc.

Don't fasten off and set aside to attach to the petal skirt later.

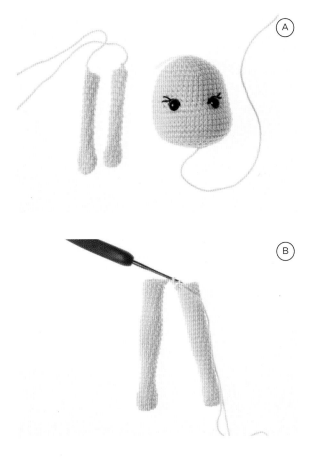

Ruffle

Use 2.5mm hook and Teddy's Wool Starlight Silver.

Connect the yarn to the FLO of Row 2, [2 dc in next st, 3 dc in next st] 18 times. (90 sts). Fasten off and weave in ends.

Skirt petals (make 18 in total)

Using 2.5mm hook, make 6 petals in each of the following colours:

Scheepjes Organicon Pink Elephant (248), Scheepjes Organicon Apple Blossom (207) and Scheepjes Organicon Pink Petunia (249).

Make a magic ring.

Round 1: 5 sc into ring. (5 sts)

Round 2: [2 sc in next st] 5 times. (10 sts)

Round 3: [2 sc in next st, 1 sc] 5 times. (15 sts)

Round 4: [2 sc in next st, 2 sc] 5 times. (20 sts)

Round 5: [2 sc in next st, 3 sc] 5 times. (25 sts)

Round 6: [2 sc in next st, 4 sc] 5 times. (30 sts)

Round 7: [2 sc in next st, 5 sc] 5 times. (35 sts)

Round 8: [4 hdc, 2 hdc in next st] 7 times. (42 sts)

Round 9: 4 dc, [2 dc in next st] 17 times, p, [2 dc in next st] 17 times, 4 dc. (76 sts + p)

(A) Fasten off and weave in ends.

Attaching the petals

Arrange your petals: 1 dark, 1 medium, 1 light, etc, with their points facing downward.

(B) (C) (D) Using 2.5mm hook and Scheepjes Organicon Pink Petunia (249), connect the yarn to the first st of one of the petals.

Row 1: 2 sc into the first 2 sts only of each petal; repeat in all the petals. (36 sts). Turn, ch 1.

Row 2: [8 sc, 2 sc in next st] 4 times. (40 sts). Fasten off and weave in ends.

Attaching the skirt to the top

(E) (F) (G) Place the wrong sides of the top and skirt facing each other, 40 slst through the BLO of the top and skirt to crochet them together.

Fasten off and weave in ends.

Little roses

(H) Using 2.25mm hook and Scheepjes Organicon Pink Elephant (248), ch 19.

Row 1: Skip last 2 sts of ch, [1 dc, 2 dc in next st] 2 times, 1 dc, ch 2, slst in next st, ch 2, [1 hdc, 2 hdc in next st] 2 times, 1 hdc, ch 2, slst into next sts, ch 1, [1 sc, 2 sc in next st] 2 times, slst in last st to fasten off.

Leave a long tail, roll up the rose and sew together tightly. You can attach the roses to the doll's hair buns, skirt, and feet.

Little Bee Friend

Finished size: 5.5cm (2⅛in)

YARNS

Krea Deluxe Organic Cotton 20, Krea Deluxe Organic Cotton 06, Scheepjes Organicon Ebony (218)

HOOK

2.25mm

Head and body

Using 2.25mm hook and Scheepjes Organicon Ebony (218), make a magic ring.

Round 1: 6 sc into ring. (6 sts)

Round 2: [2 sc in next st] 6 times. (12 sts)

Round 3: [3 sc in next st, 5 sc] 2 times. (16 sts)

Rounds 4 to 6: 16 sc.

Insert 4mm safety eyes between Rounds 3 and 4 on either side of the Bee's head. You might have to shorten the stems of the eyes so they fit into the head.

Round 7: [invdec] 8 times. (8 sts). Stuff the head well.

Switch to Krea Deluxe Organic Cotton 06.

(A) Round 8: ch 2, [2 3tr-cl in next st, 1 3tr-cl] 4 times, slst into first st to close. (12 sts)

Switch to Scheepjes Organicon Ebony (218).

Round 9: ch 2, 12 3tr-cl, slst into first st to close. (12 sts). Switch to Krea Deluxe Organic Cotton 06.

Round 10: Repeat Round 9.

Switch to Scheepjes Organicon Ebony (218).

(B) Round 11: Repeat Round 9.

Stuff firmly.

Round 12: 12 sc.

Round 13: [invdec] 6 times. (6 sts)

(C) Close, fasten off and pull out the yarn to create the stinger.

Antennae

Using Scheepjes Organicon Ebony (218), cut a 5cm (2in) piece of yarn and pull it through the top of the Bee's head making a small knot at each end for the antenna.

Wings (make 2)

Using 2.25mm hook and Krea Deluxe Organic Cotton 20, make a magic ring.

Round 1: 8 sc into ring. (8 sts)

Round 2: [3 sc in next st, 3 sc] 2 times. (12 sts)

Round 3: [3 sc in next st, 5 sc] 2 times. (16 sts)

Rounds 4 to 8: 16 sc.

Round 9: [invdec, 6 sc] 2 times. (14 sts)

Round 10: [invdec, 5 sc] 2 times. (12 sts)

Round 11: [invdec, 4 sc] 2 times. (10 sts)

Round 12: [invdec, 3 sc] 2 times. (8 sts)

Set aside to connect to the second wing later.

Ⓓ Ⓔ Create the second wing. Then place the wings on top of each other and sc through both to connect them.

Fasten off and leave a long tail to sew onto Round 4 of the Bee's body.

Ⓐ

Ⓑ

Ⓒ

Ⓓ

Ⓔ
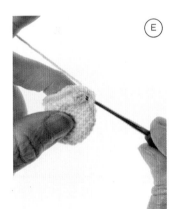

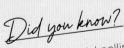
Did you know?

Bees are essential pollinators responsible for one-third of the food we eat! These tiny superheroes visit flowers to collect nectar and pollen, transferring pollen grains between flowers to help plants reproduce. Bees live in highly organised colonies, with each bee having a specific role like foraging, nursing, and protecting the hive. Their intricate dance, known as the waggle dance, communicates the location of food sources to other bees. Protecting bees ensures our food supply and supports biodiversity worldwide.

Mushroom Sprite & Hedgehog

The Mushroom Sprite watches over the forest floor, bringing a touch of magic to the woods. She ensures the health and balance of fungal ecosystems, from delicate mushrooms to towering fungi and symbiotic mycorrhizal networks.

Fungi are vital components of ecosystems worldwide, playing essential roles in decomposition, nutrient cycling, and symbiotic relationships with plants. They break down organic matter, recycle nutrients, and support plant growth, contributing to soil health and productivity. Fungi are also used in medicine, food production, and biotechnology, highlighting their diverse and indispensable contributions to human well-being.

Celebrating the Mushroom Sprite means appreciating the hidden wonders of the forest and the crucial role mushrooms play in its vitality.

DIFFICULTY LEVEL: EASY

Mushroom Sprite

Finished size: 10cm (4in)

YARNS

Krea Deluxe Organic Cotton 46, Scheepjes Organicon Broken Almond (220), Scheepjes Organicon Cherry Jam (243), Scheepjes Organicon Oat Bath (242), Teddy's Wool Starlight Silver

HOOKS

2.25mm, 2.5mm

(A) Arms and head

Using 2.25mm hook and Scheepjes Organicon Broken Almond (220), make the arms using the general pattern instructions (see Making the basic doll) and stop after Round 10.

Make the head following the small head instructions (see Making the basic doll).

Feet and legs

Using 2.25mm hook and Scheepjes Organicon Broken Almond (220), ch 4.

Round 1: Skip last st of ch, 2 sc into one side of ch, 3 sc into first st of ch, 2 sc into opposite side of ch. (7 sts)

Place marker.

Round 2: 3 sc into first st, 2 sc, 3 sc in next st, 3 sc. (11 sts)

Round 3: 11 sc.

Create the heel by working back and forth, do not ch 1 after turn.

Row 4: 7 sc, turn, sc2tog, 2 sc, sc2tog.

Continue working in the round.

Round 5: Turn, 4 sc, 1 sc into space between heel and top of foot, 6 sc into top of foot, 1 sc into space between top of foot and heel. (12 sts)

Place marker.

Round 6: 4 sc, invdec, 4 sc, invdec. (10 sts)

Rounds 7 to 10: 10 sc.

Fasten off and set aside to attach to second leg later. Make second leg the same through to Round 10, then work 6 sc to move to joining point.

Round 11: 6 sc, ch 2, connect by 10 sc around first leg, starting after the fastened-off st, 2 sc into ch, 10 sc around second leg, 2 sc into opposite side of ch. (24 sts)

NOTE: Adjust sts if necessary to make sure both feet are facing forward by sc more or fewer sts around the legs in Round 10.

Place marker.

Body

Continue working in the round for body.

Round 1: [1 sc, 2 sc in next st] 2 times, 14 sc, [2 sc in next st, 1 sc] 2 times, 2 sc. (28 sts)

Rounds 2 and 3: 28 sc.

Stuff the tips of the toes, insert your wire frame and continue stuffing the legs.

(B) Make the torso and neck using the general pattern instructions (see Making the basic doll).

Trousers

C — Using 2.5mm hook and Krea Deluxe Organic Cotton 46, ch 12, slst in first st to form a circle, taking care not to twist your stitches.

Round 1: 12 sc in ch.

Place marker.

Round 2: BLO [2 sc in next st] 12 times. (24 sts)

Rounds 3 and 4: 24 sc.

Fasten off and set aside to connect to second leg.

Make second trouser leg the same through to Round 4, don't fasten off.

Round 5: Connect both legs by working 24 sc around first leg and working 24 sc around second leg. (48 sts)

Rounds 6 to 9: 48 sc.

Round 10: [1 sc, invdec] 16 times. (32 sts)

Round 11: 32 sc.

Round 12: BLO 32 hdc. Fasten off and weave in ends.

Straps

Ch 20, skip last st of ch, 19 sc into ch.

Fasten off and sew straps onto front of overalls, cross them in the back and sew them onto the back.

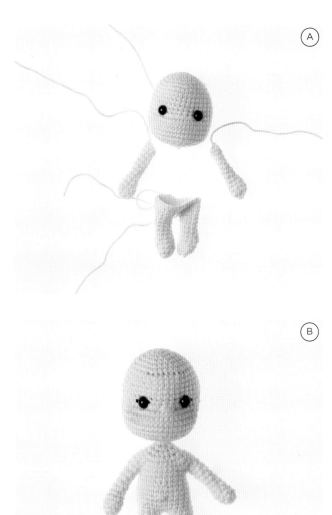

A

B

C

Mushroom hat

Using 2.5mm hook and Scheepjes Organicon Cherry Jam (243), make a magic ring.

Round 1: 6 sc into ring. (6 sts)

Round 2: [2 sc in next st] 6 times. (12 sts)

Round 3: [2 sc in next st, 1 sc] 6 times. (18 sts)

Round 4: [2 sc in next st, 2 sc] 6 times. (24 sts)

Round 5: [2 sc in next st, 3 sc] 6 times. (30 sts)

Round 6: [2 sc in next st, 4 sc] 6 times. (36 sts)

Round 7: [2 sc in next st, 5 sc] 6 times. (42 sts)

Rounds 8 to 13: 42 sc.

Round 14: [2 sc in next st, 2 sc] 14 times. (56 sts)

Round 15: [2 sc in next st, 3 sc] 14 times. (70 sts)

Rounds 16 to 19: 70 sc.

Round 20: [5 sc, invdec] 10 times. (60 sts)

Switch to Scheepjes Organicon Oat Bath (242).

Round 21: BLO 60 hdc.

Round 22: [4 sc, invdec] 10 times. (50 sts)

(A) **Rounds 19 to 24:** BLO 50 hdc.

Round 25: [3 sc, invdec] 10 times. (40 sts)

Round 26: 40 sc.

Round 27: [2 sc, invdec] 10 times. (30 sts)

(B) **Round 28:** [1 sc, invdec] 10 times. (20 sts)

Stuff the inside of the mushroom top and rim very, very lightly. Take care not to overstuff!

Round 29: [invdec] 10 times. (10 sts)

Round 30: [invdec] 5 times. (5 sts)

(C) Close, fasten off and weave in ends. Push the beige-coloured part inside the hat. Sew the hat onto the doll's head.

(D) Dots (make 7)

(E) Using 2.25mm hook and Teddy's Wool Starlight Silver, make a magic ring.

Round 1: 6 sc into ring. (6 sts)

Fasten off, leave a long tail and sew onto the hat. You can also add some bullion stitches in Teddy's Wool Starlight Silver.

Little Hedgehog Friend

Finished size: 3cm (1¼in)

YARNS

Krea Deluxe Organic Cotton 29, Krea Deluxe Organic Cotton 18, Krea Deluxe Organic Cotton 51, Krea Deluxe Organic Cotton 46, Scheepjes Organicon Aloeswood (241)

HOOKS

2mm, 2.25mm

Bag

Using 2.25mm hook and Scheepjes Organicon Aloeswood (241), ch 13.

Round 1: Skip last st of ch, 11 sc into one side of ch, 3 sc into last sts of ch, 11 sc into opposite side of ch. (25 sts)

Round 2: 3 sc in first st, 11 sc, 3 sc in next st, 12 sc. (29 sts)

Rounds 3 to 10: 29 sc

(A) **Round 11:** ch 22, skip 14 sts, 1 sc, 22 sc into ch.

Fasten off and weave in ends.

Hedgehog

Head

Using 2mm hook and Krea Deluxe Organic Cotton 18, make a magic ring.

Round 1: 5 sc into ring. (5 sts)

Round 2: 5 sc.

Round 3: [2 sc in next st] 3 times, 2 sc. (8 sts)

Round 4: 3 sc in next st, [2 sc in next st] 3 times, 3 sc in next st, 3 sc. (15 sts)

Round 5: 1 sc, 2 sc in next st, 3 sc in next st, 6 sc, 3 sc in next st, 2 sc in next st, 4 sc. (21 sts)

Round 6: 21 sc.

Fasten off and weave in ends. Set aside to attach to body later.

Body

Using 2mm hook and Krea Deluxe Organic Cotton 18, make a magic ring.

Round 1: 6 sc into ring. (6 sts)

Round 2: [2 sc in next st] 6 times. (12 sts)

Round 3: [2 sc in next st, 1 sc] 6 times. (18 sts)

Round 4: [2 sc in next st, 2 sc] 6 times. (24 sts)

Did you know?

Hedgehogs are adorable mammals known for their unique defense mechanism: When threatened, they curl into a tight ball, using their spiky quills as armour. These nocturnal creatures are excellent pest controllers, feeding on insects, snails, and even small vertebrates. Hedgehogs play a crucial role in garden ecosystems by keeping insect populations in check. Despite their solitary nature, they are surprisingly vocal, using various grunts, snuffles, and squeals to communicate. Hedgehogs hibernate during winter to conserve energy, relying on fat reserves built up during the warmer months.

Connecting the head and body

Hold the head and body together, right sides facing.

Round 4: 4 sc through the body and the head, stop round here. Fasten off and leave a long tail to sew onto the pompom later.

Using 1 strand of Krea Deluxe Organic Cotton 18 and 2 strands of Krea Deluxe Organic Cotton 51 together, make a mini pompom (about 5cm (2in) in circumference).

Sew the body onto the pompom (you can glue it if you prefer), then trim the pompom into a cute round shape.

With black embroidery yarn, sew a little nose and eyelids onto the face of the Hedgehog using the picture to guide you.

Place the Hedgehog inside the little bag.

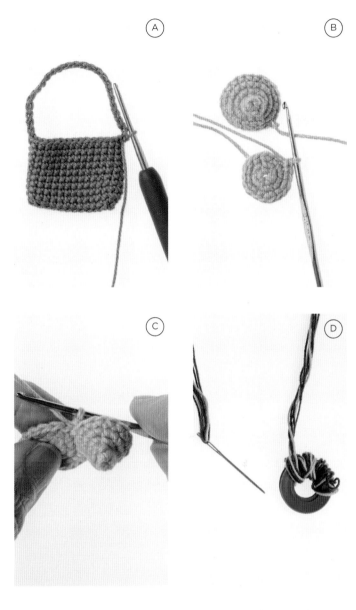

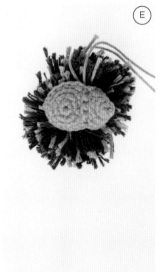

Insect Lord & Firefly

The Insect Lord reigns over the world of insects, where every tiny creature plays a significant role in the ecosystem. He ensures the balance and vitality of insect populations, from industrious bees to graceful butterflies and diligent ants. As the protector of tiny marvels, the Insect Prince plays a crucial role in maintaining the intricate web of life on Earth.

Insects are essential for ecosystem function and human well-being in countless ways. They pollinate crops, allowing for the production of fruits, vegetables, and seeds. Insects also decompose organic matter, recycling nutrients back into the soil and supporting plant growth. Furthermore, they serve as a crucial food source for many species, including birds, bats, and amphibians.

The Insect Lord symbolises the often-overlooked but indispensable role of insects in sustaining life on our planet. By honouring the Insect lord, we celebrate the diversity and resilience of these small but mighty creatures and recognise their critical importance in maintaining healthy ecosystems worldwide.

DIFFICULTY LEVEL: ADVANCED

Insect Lord

Finished size: 22cm (8¾in)

YARNS

Scheepjes Organicon Hickory (240), Scheepjes Organicon Wild Nectarine (221), Scheepjes Organicon Aloeswood (241), Scheepjes Organicon Fossil (262), Scheepjes Organicon Ashen Mink (201), Scheepjes Organicon Maple Bark (226), Teddy's Wool Starlight Silver

HOOK

2.25mm

(A) Arms and head

Use 2.25mm hook and Scheepjes Organicon Wild Nectarine (221).

Make the arms and large head using the general pattern instructions (see Making the basic doll). You can add some freckles with acrylic paint.

Feet and legs

Using 2.25mm hook and Scheepjes Organicon Wild Nectarine (221), ch 4.

Round 1: Skip last st of ch, 2 sc into one side of ch, 3 sc into first st of ch, 2 sc into opposite side of ch. (7 sts)

Place marker.

Round 2: 3 sc into first st, 2 sc, 3 sc in next st, 3 sc. (11 sts)

Round 3: 11 sc.

Create the heel by working back and forth, do not ch 1 after turn.

Row 4: 7 sc, turn, sc2tog, 2 sc, sc2tog. Turn.

Continue working in the round.

(B) Round 5: 4 sc, 1 sc into space between heel and top of foot, 6 sc into top of foot, 1 sc into space between top of foot and heel. (12 sts)

Place marker.

Round 6: 4 sc, invdec, 4 sc, invdec. (10 sts)

Rounds 7 to 12: 10 sc.

Round 13: [2 sc in next st, 4 sc] 2 times. (12 sts)

Switch to Scheepjes Organicon Aloeswood (241).

Rounds 14 and 15: 12 sc.

Round 16: 11 sc, 2 sc in next st. (13 sts)

Rounds 17 to 33: 13 sc.

Round 34: 6 sc, stop here.

Fasten off and set aside to attach to second leg later. Make second leg the same through to Round 33, then work 12 sc to move to joining point

(C) Round 34: Ch 2, connect by 13 sc around first leg, starting after the fastened-off st, 2 sc into ch, 13 sc around second leg, 2 sc into opposite side of ch. (30 sts)

NOTE: Adjust sts if necessary to make sure both feet are facing forward by sc more or fewer sts around the legs in Round 34.

Place marker.

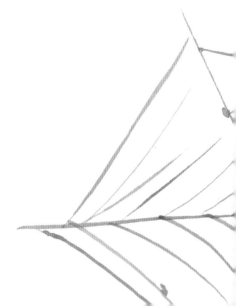

Body

Continue working in the round for body.

Round 1: 2 sc, 2 sc in next st, 1 sc, 2 sc in next st, 19 sc, 2 sc in next st, 1 sc, 2 sc in next st, 3 sc. (34 sts)

Rounds 2 to 7: 34 sc.

Stuff the tips of the toes, insert your wire frame, continue stuffing the legs.

Round 8: 7 sc, invdec, 15 sc, invdec, 8 sc. (32 sts)

Work torso and neck using the general pattern instructions (see Making the basic doll).

Ears (make 2)

Using 2.25mm hook and Scheepjes Wild Nectarine (221), make a magic ring.

Round 1: ch 2, 1 dc, 4 sc, p, 1 sc in ring.

Fasten off and leave a long tail. Sew the ears on either side of the doll's head, centering them between Rounds 13 and 14, 5 sts away from the eyes.

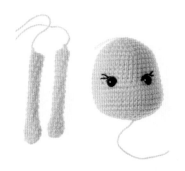

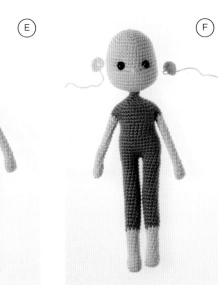

Hair

Use 2.25mm hook and Scheepjes Fossil (262).

Measure out about 5cm (2in) of yarn and create the hair following the general instructions (see Making the basic doll), making hair strands of 1 to 2 sts.

Antennae (make 2)

Using 2.25mm hook and Scheepjes Organicon Fossil (262), ch 14.

Row 1: Skip last 2 sts of ch, 12 hdc into ch.

Repeat ch 14 and Row 1, then sew the two pieces together all around with a simple running st, for more stability. Leave a long piece of yarn to sew the antenna onto the doll's head.

(A)
(B) Cut a 2cm (¾in) piece of yarn and fold it in half to form a loop. Insert your hook into a BLO of the ch, pull the loop through, pull the ends of the yarn though the loop on your hook and tighten.

(C) Repeat on both sides of the ch and on the top sts of the chain. Brush the edges of the yarn out with a pet brush (or fine-toothed comb) until fluffy.

Sew the antennae onto the top of the doll's head, about 7 Rounds above the ears.

Crown

Using 2.25mm hook and Teddy's Wool Starlight Silver, ch 42, slst in first st to form a circle, taking care not to twist the sts.

Round 1: 42 sc into ch.

Round 2: [ch 1, skip next st, 1 hdc] 21 times.

Fasten off and weave in ends. Place on the doll's head.

Boots

Using 2.25mm hook and Scheepjes Organicon Hickory (240), ch 4.

Round 1: Skip last st of ch, 2 sc in one side of ch, 3 sc into first sts of ch, 2 sc in opposite side of ch. (7 sts)

Place marker.

(D) **Round 2:** 3 sc in first st, 2 sc, 3 sc in next st, 3 sc. (11 sts)

Round 3: 1 sc, [3 sc in next st, 4 sc] 2 times. (15 sts)

Round 4: 1 sc, *[2 sc in next st] 3 times, 4 sc; repeat from * 2 times. (21 sts)

(E) Trace the sole on a piece of cardboard, cut it out and save to insert into the boot for more stability. This step is optional.

Round 5: BLO 21 sc.

Rounds 6 and 7: 21 sc.

Round 8: [invdec] 4 times, 13 sts. (17 sts)

Round 9: [invdec] 2 times, 13 sc. (15 sts). Insert the soles into the boot.

Rounds 10 to 17: 15 sc.

Fasten off, weave in ends and place on the doll's feet. Use the chart to embroider pattern onto outside of boots using cross stitch. Each square on the chart corresponds with one crochet stitch.

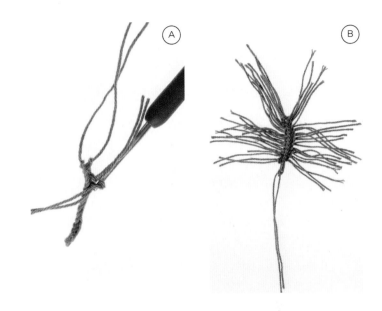

Embroidery pattern for boots

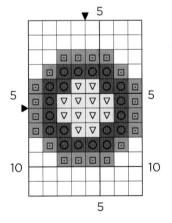

▽ A Teddy's Wool Starlight Silver

◉ B Scheepjes Organicon Maple Bark (226)

▣ C Scheepjes Organicon Aloeswood (241)

Cardigan

Yarn quantity: 30g (1oz)

(A) The cardigan is worked back and forth in rows. Turn and ch after each row (ch counts as st). Using Scheepjes Organicon Hickory (240), ch 32.

Row 1: Skip last 2 sts of ch, 29 dc. (30 sts) Turn, ch 2.

Row 2: FLO [2 dc, 2 dc in next st] 10 times. (40 sts). Turn, ch 2.

Row 3: [ch 1, skip 1 dc, 1 dc in next st] 20 times. (20 sts + 19 ch sps). Turn, ch 2.

Row 4: [1 dc in ch 1 space, 1 dc] 20 times. (40 sts). Turn, ch 2.

Rows 5 and 6: Repeat Rounds 3 and 4. Turn, ch 2.

Row 7: Repeat Round 3.

(B) **Row 8:** [1 dc in ch 1 space, 1 dc] 3 times, ch 4, [skip next ch space, skip next dc] 2 times, [1 dc in ch 1 space, 1 dc] 9 times, ch 4, [skip next ch 1 space, skip next dc] 2 times, [1 dc in ch 1 space, 1 dc] 3 times. Turn, ch 2.

Row 9: 5 dc, 5 dc in ch 4 space, 18 dc, 5 dc in ch 4 sp, 6 dc. (40 sts). Turn, ch 2.

Row 10: [2 dec, invdec] 10 times. (30 sts) Turn, do not ch 2.

Row 11: 4 slst, ch 2 (counts as 1 dc), 19 dc. Stop Round here. (20 sts). Turn, ch 2.

Row 12: 19 dc. Turn, ch 1.

Row 13: 19 sc.

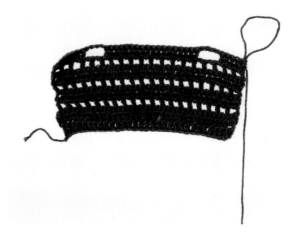

Fasten off and weave in ends.

Place on your doll and turn the collar down.

Belt

The belt is worked back and forth in rows. Turn and ch after each row (ch counts as a st). Using Scheepjes Organicon Hickory (240), ch 51.

Row 1: Skip last st of chain, 50 sc into ch. (50 sts). Turn, ch 2.

Row 2: [ch 1, skip next st, 1 hdc] 25 times. Fasten off and weave in ends.

(C) Tie around the doll's waist.

Wings

Top wings

Using 2.25mm hook and Scheepjes Organicon Ashen Mink (201), ch 5.

Round 1: Skip first st of ch, 3 sc into one side of ch, 3 sc into first st of ch, 3 sc into opposite side of ch. (9 sts)

Place marker.

Round 2: 3 sc in first st, 3 sc, 3 sc in next st, 4 sc. (13 sts)

Round 3: 1 sc, 3 sc in next st, 5 sc, 3 sc in next st, 5 sc. (17 sts)

Round 4: 2 sc, 3 sc in next st, 7 sc, 3 sc in next st, 6 sc. (21 sts)

Round 5: 3 sc, 3 sc in next st, 9 sc, 3 sc in next st, 7 sc. (25 sts)

Round 6: 4 sc, 3 sc in first st, 11 sc, 3 sc in next st, 8 sc. (29 sts)

Round 7: 5 sc, 3 sc in next st, 13 sc, 3 sc in next st, 9 sc. (33 sts)

Round 8: 6 sc, 3 sc in next st, 15 sc, 3 sc in next st, 10 sc. (37 sts)

Round 9: 7 sc, 3 sc in next st, 17 sc, 3 sc in next st, 11 sc. (41 sts)

Round 10: 8 sc, 3 sc in next st, 19 sc, 3 sc in next st, 12 sc. (45 sts)

Rounds 11 to 27: 43 sc.

Round 28: 8 sc, sc3tog, 34 sc. (43 sts)

Round 29: 7 sc, sc3tog, 33 sc. (41 sts)

Round 30: 6 sc, sc3tog, 32 sc. (39 sts)

Round 31: 5 sc, sc3tog, 31 sc. (37 sts)

Round 32: 4 sc, sc3tog, 16 sc, sc3tog, 11 sc. (33 sts)

Round 33: 3 sc, sc3tog, 14 sc, sc3tog, 10 sc. (29 sts)

Round 34: 2 sc, sc3tog, 12 sc, sc3tog, 9 sc. (25 sts)

Round 35: 1 sc, sc3tog, 10 sc, sc3tog, 8 sc. (21 sts)

Round 36: sc3tog, 8 sc, sc3tog, 7 sc. (17 sts)

Round 37: 7 sc BLO into both sides together to close.

Fasten off and leave a long tail to sew onto the coat. Use the chart to embroider pattern onto outside of wings using cross stitch. Each square on the chart corresponds with one crochet stitch.

Ⓐ Bottom wings

Using 2.25mm hook and Teddy's Wool Starlight Silver, make a magic ring.

Round 1: 6 sc into ring. (6 sts)

Round 2: [2 sc in next st] 6 times. (12 sts)

Switch to Scheepjes Organicon Aloeswood (241).

Round 3: BLO [2 sc in next st, 1 sc] 6 times, ch 6, skip last st of ch, 5 sc into ch. (29 sts)

Place marker.

Round 4: [2 sc in next st, 2 sc] 6 times, 5 sc into ch, 3 sc in next st, 5 sc along other side of ch. (37 sts)

Round 5: [2 sc in next st, 3 sc] 5 times, 10 sc, 3 sc in next st, 6 sc. (44 sts)

Switch to Scheepjes Organicon Fossil (262).

Round 6: BLO [2 sc in next st, 4 sc] 5 times, 11 sc, 3 sc in next st, 7 sc. (51 sts)

Round 7: 42 sc, 3 sc in next st, 8 sc. (53 sts)

Embroidery pattern for top wings

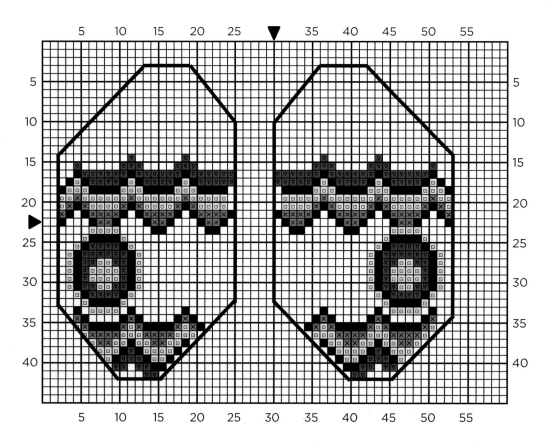

A Teddy's Wool Starlight Silver

B Scheepjes Organicon Fossil (262)

C Scheepjes Organicon Maple Bark (226)

D Scheepjes Organicon Hickory (240)

Switch to Scheepjes Organicon Maple Bark (226).

Round 8: BLO [5 sc, 2 sc in next st] 5 times, 13 sc, 3 sc in next st, 9 sc. (60 sts)

Round 9: [6 sc, 2 sc in next st] 5 times, 14 sc, 3 sc in next st, 10 sc. (67 sts)

Round 10: [7 sc, 2 sc in next st] 5 times, 15 sc, 3 sc in next st, 11 sc. (74 sts)

Round 11: [8 sc, 2 sc in next st] 5 times, 16 sc, 3 sc in next st, 12 sc. (81 sts)

Round 12: [9 sc, 2 sc in next st] 5 times, 17 sc, 3 sc in next st, 13 sc. (88 sts)

Switch to Teddy's Wool Starlight Silver.

Round 13: 88 sc.

Fasten off and weave in ends. Sew onto the doll's coat, 2 rows under the top wings.

Wire rim glasses

Using 0.5mm (24 gauge) wire, curve the end slightly, then measure from left ear to left eye, twist the wire around a dowel or pencil, continue straight to right eye, twist around a dowel or pencil again, fold around to right ear, curve the end slightly and cut the wire. Make sure the cut ends are not sharp. See Templates for full-size template.

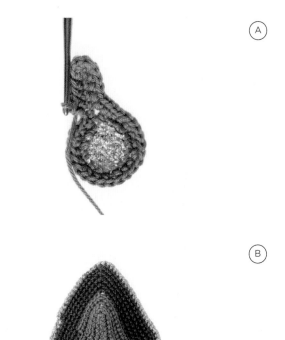

Little Firefly Friend

Finished size: 3.5cm (1⅜in)

YARNS

Krea Deluxe Organic Cotton 51, Scheepjes Organicon Maple Bark (226), Scheepjes Organicon Ebony (218), glow-in-the-dark embroidery yarn (floss)

HOOKS

2mm, 2.25mm

Head and body

Using 2mm hook and Scheepjes Organicon Maple Bark (226), make a magic ring.

Round 1: 6 sc into ring. (6 sts)

Round 2: [2 sc in next st] 6 times. (12 sts)

Round 3: [2 sc in next st, 5 sc] 2 times. (14 sts)

Rounds 4 and 5: 14 sc.

Insert 7mm safety eyes between Rounds 3 and 4 on either side of the Firefly's head. You might have to shorten the stems of the eyes so they fit into the head.

Round 6: [invdec] 7 times. (7 sts). Stuff the head well.

Round 7: [2 sc in next st] 7 times. (14 sts)

Switch to glow-in-the-dark embroidery yarn.

Ⓐ **Round 8:** BLO [2 sc in next st, 6 sc] 2 times. (16 sts)

Rounds 9 to 11: BLO 16 sc.

Round 12: BLO [invdec, 6 sc] 2 times. (14 sts)

Round 13: [invdec] 7 times. (7 sts)

Ⓑ Don't stuff! Close, fasten off and weave in ends.

Wings

Top wings (make 2)

Using 2.25mm hook and Scheepjes Organicon Ebony (218), make a magic ring.

Round 1: 6 sc into ring. (6 sts)

Round 2: [2 sc in next st, 2 sc] 2 times. (8 sts)

Rounds 3 to 8: 8 sc.

Fasten off and weave in ends. Set aside to attach to bottom wings.

Bottom wings

Using 2.25mm hook and Krea Deluxe Organic Cotton 51, ch 8, slst in first st to form a circle, taking care not to twist your sts.

Ⓒ **Round 1:** 10 sc around circle. (10 sts)

Round 2: ch 8, slst in first st to form a circle.

Round 3: 10 sc around circle.

Ⓓ **Round 4:** ch 8, slst into 6th st of first loop.

Round 5: ch 1, turn, 10 sc around loop, slst into first st.

Ⓔ Repeat Rounds 4 and 5 on the other loop to create the second half of wing. Fasten off and weave in ends.

Did you know?

Fireflies, also known as lightning bugs, create their magical glow through a chemical reaction called bioluminescence. This enchanting light show is used to attract mates and communicate. Fireflies are important for ecosystems, as their larvae help control pest populations by feeding on other insects. These tiny, twinkling creatures remind us of nature's wonders and the delicate balance within our environments.

Connecting the wings

(F) Take one of the top wings, pinch the opening
closed, 1 sc through both halves of this wing.
(G) Take the second top wing, pinch the opening
closed then take the narrow part of the bottom
wing and 2 sc through all wings to connect
them. Finish with 1 sc through both halves of the
first top wing.

Fasten off and leave a long tail. Sew the wings
onto the body. Weave in ends.

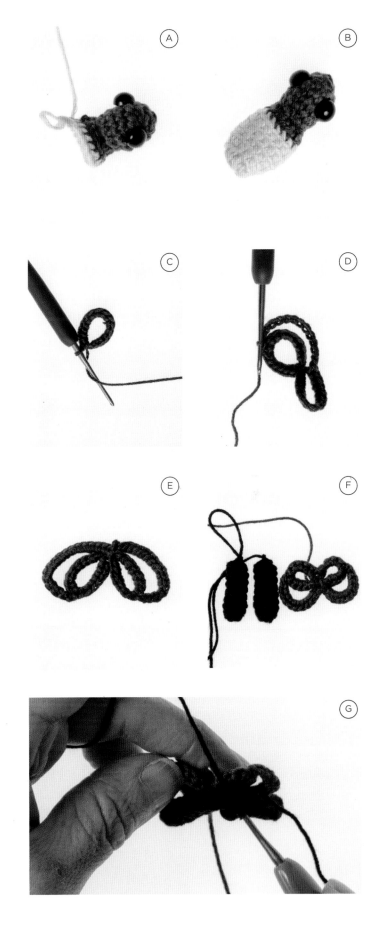

Sun Queen
& Iguana

The Sun Queen reigns over sun-drenched landscapes, embodying the strength and resilience of the desert. She brings life to the arid terrain, ensuring that even the harshest environments teem with beauty and vitality. Her warmth nurtures unique flora and fauna, from hardy cacti to swift lizards.

As the protector of radiant light, the Sun Queen plays a crucial role in driving photosynthesis, supporting plant growth, and regulating temperatures. She embodies sunlit majesty, maintaining the delicate balance of the desert ecosystem, showcasing nature's adaptability and wonder. By honouring the Sun Queen's realm, we celebrate the stark yet vibrant beauty of the desert and the life it sustains.

DIFFICULTY LEVEL: EASY

Sun Queen

Finished size: 22cm (8¾in)

YARNS

Scheepjes Organicon Mellow Mustard (236), Scheepjes Organicon Buttermilk (210), Scheepjes Organicon Gentle Primrose (211), Scheepjes Organicon Golden Sun (237), Teddy's Wool Starlight Silver

HOOKS

2.25mm, 2.5mm

Arms and head

Use 2.25mm hook and Scheepjes Organicon Mellow Mustard (236).

(A) Make the arms and large head using the general pattern instructions (see Making the basic doll).

Lashes

Embroider 2 small lashes on the outside of the eyes.

Then make the legs and lower body following the instructions below:

Feet and legs

Using 2.25mm hook and Scheepjes Organicon Mellow Mustard (236), ch 3.

Round 1: Skip last st of ch, 1 sc into one side of ch, 3 sc into first st of ch, 1 sc into opposite side of ch. (5 sts)

Place marker.

Round 2: 3 sc into first st, 1 sc, 3 sc in next st, 2 sc. (9 sts)

Round 3: 9 sc.

Create the heel by working back and forth, do not ch 1 after turn.

Row 4: 5 sc, turn, sc2tog, 1 sc, sc2tog, turn.

Continue working in the round.

Round 5: 3 sc, 1 sc into space between heel and top of foot, 5 sc into top of foot, 1 sc into space between top of foot and heel. (10 sts)

Place marker.

Round 6: [3 sc, invdec] 2 times. (8 sts)

Rounds 7 to 9: 8 sc.

(B) **Round 10:** [2 sc in next st, 3 sc] 2 times. (10 sts)

Rounds 11 to 15: 10 sc.

Round 16: [2 sc in next st, 4 sc] 2 times. (12 sts)

Rounds 17 to 28: 12 sc.

Round 29: 6 sc. Stop Round here.

Fasten off and set aside to attach to second leg later. Make second leg the same through to Round 28.

(C) **Round 29:** Ch 2, connect by 12 sc around first leg, starting after the fastened-off st, 2 sc into ch, 12 sc around second leg, 2 sc into opposite side of ch. (28 sts)

NOTE: Adjust sts if necessary to make sure both feet are facing forward by sc more or fewer sts around the legs in Round 29.

Place marker.

Body

Continue working in the round for body.

Round 1: [1 sc, 2 sc in next st] 2 times, 18 sc, [2 sc in next st, 1 sc] 2 times, 2 sc. (32 sts)

Rounds 2 to 6: 32 sc.

Stuff the tips of the toes, insert your wire frame and continue stuffing the legs.

(D)
(E) Make torso and neck using the general pattern instructions (see Making the basic doll).

F Hair

Yarn quantity: 50g (1¾oz)

Using 2.25mm hook and Scheepjes Organicon Buttermilk (210), measure about 96cm (38in) and create the hair following the general instructions (see Making the basic doll), making hair strands of 35 to 45 sts.

To make the curly ends:

After you make your chain, don't cut the yarn and continue working with the long strand, ch 1, [2 sc into next st of ch, 3 sc] 3 times, slst to fasten off.

Weave in end.

G H Ears

Using 2.25mm hook and Scheepjes Organicon Mellow Mustard (236), make a magic ring.

Round 1: Ch 2, 1 dc, 5 hdc, slst into ring. Fasten off and weave in ends.

Sew the ears onto the sides of the doll's head between Rounds 12 and 14, 5 sts away from the eyes.

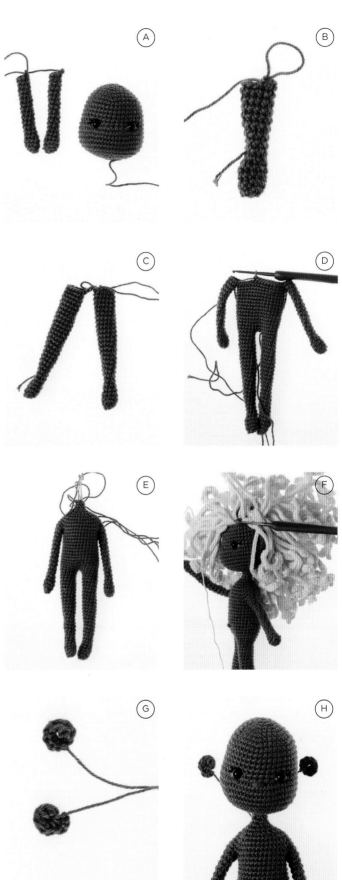

Overalls

Yarn quantity: 50g (1¾oz)

The overalls are made by crocheting back and forth in rows. Turn and ch after each row (ch does not count as st).

When switching colours, don't cut the yarn but bring it up loosely at the side of your work. All rows are worked in BLO.

Bottom of overalls

Using 2.5mm hook and Scheepjes Organicon Golden Sun (237), ch 40.

Row 1: Skip last st of ch, 7 sc, 32 hdc. (39 sts) Turn, ch 2.

(A) **Row 2:** BLO 32 hdc, 7 sc. (39 sts). Turn, ch 1.

Switch to Scheepjes Organicon Gentle Primrose (211).

Row 3: BLO 7 sc, 32 hdc. (39 sts). Turn, ch 2.

Row 4: BLO 32 hdc, 7 sc. (39 sts). Turn, ch 1.

Switch to Scheepjes Organicon Golden Sun (237).

Row 5: BLO 7 sc, 32 hdc. (39 sts). Turn, ch 2.

Row 6: BLO 32 hdc, 7 sc. (39 sts). Turn, ch 1.

Rows 7 to 14: Repeat Rows 3 to 6, twice.

Rows 15 and 16: Repeat Rows 3 and 4.

Switch to Scheepjes Organicon Golden Sun (237).

(B) **Row 17:** 7 sc, 10 hdc, ch 24. (17 sts + 24 ch)

Row 18: Skip last 2 sts of ch, 22 hdc in ch, 10 hdc, 7 sc. (39 sts). Turn, ch 1.

Switch to Scheepjes Organicon Gentle Primrose (211).

Row 19: BLO 7 sc, 32 hdc. (39 sts). Turn, ch 2.

Row 20: BLO 32 hdc, 7 sc. (39 sts). Turn, ch 1.

Switch to Scheepjes Organicon Golden Sun (237).

Row 21: BLO 7 sc, 32 hdc. (39 sts). Turn, ch 2.

Row 22: BLO 32 hdc, 7 sc. (39 sts). Turn, ch 1.

Rows 23 to 30: Repeat Rows 19 to 22, twice.

(C) **Rows 31 and 32:** Repeat Rows 19 and 20.

Fasten off.

Top of overalls

(D) Hold the bottom of the overalls with the first st facing upwards. Using 2.5mm hook and Scheepjes Organicon Gentle Primrose (211), reconnect your yarn to the first st of Row 1.

Row 1: 32 sc into the first/last st. Turn, ch 1.

(E) **Row 2:** 5 sc, ch 7, skip next 5 sts, sc2tog, 8 sc, sc2tog, ch 7, skip next 5 sts, 5 sc. (20 sts + 2 times 7 ch). Turn, ch 1.

Row 3: sc2tog, 3 sc, 8 sc around ch, BLO [4 sc, sc2tog, 4 sc], 8 sc around ch, 3 sc, sc2tog. (33 sts)

Turn, ch 2.

(F) Make the ruffle:

Row 4: FLO [3 dc in next st, 2 dc in next st] 16 times, 3 dc in next st. (83 sts). Turn, ch 1.

(G) Switch to Teddy's Wool Starlight Silver.

Row 5: 83 sc.

Fasten off and weave in ends.

(H) Sew the back seam from the trouser opening to the top of the overalls, then close the inseam.

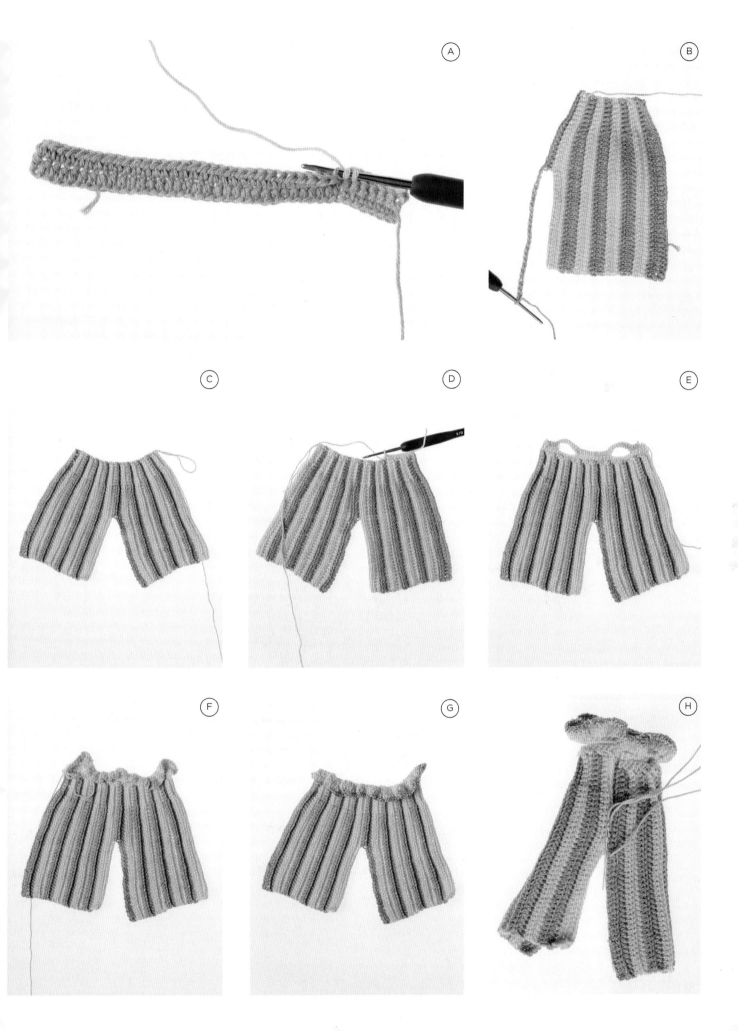

Earrings (make 2)

 Using 2.25mm hook and Scheepjes Organicon Happy Sunflower (238), ch 8, slst in first st to form a circle, taking care not to twist your sts.

Round 1: 12 sc around ch.

Switch to Teddy's Wool Starlight Silver.

Round 2: [2 sc, p] 5 times, 2 sc, ch 4.

Fasten off and leave a long piece of yarn to sew the earrings onto the doll's earlobes.

Crown

(A)

The crown is made by crocheting back and forth in rows. Turn and ch after each row. Using 2.25mm hook and Scheepjes Organicon Happy Sunflower (238), ch 37.

Row 1: Skip last st of ch, 36 sc into ch. Turn, ch 2.

Row 2: [1 hdc, 2 hdc in next st] 36 times. (54 sts). Turn, ch 1.

Switch to Teddy's Wool Starlight Silver.

Row 3: [2 sc, p] 27 times.

Fasten off and weave in ends. Place around the doll's hair.

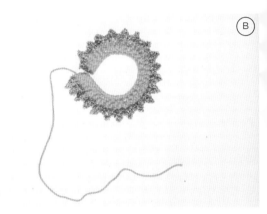

(B)

Bracelets

Using 2.25mm hook and Scheepjes Organicon Happy Sunflower (238), ch 8, slst in first st to form a circle, taking care not to twist your sts.

Round 1: 12 sc around ch. Fasten off and weave in ends.

Make another bracelet using Teddy's Wool Starlight Silver, place on your doll's arms.

Little Iguana Friend

Finished size: 10.5cm (4⅛in)

YARNS

Scheepjes Organicon Sweet Mandarin (223),
Scheepjes Organicon Curly Dock (225)

HOOK

2.25mm

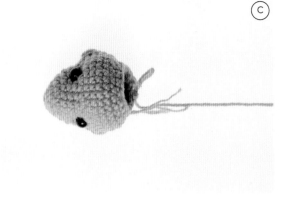

Head and body

Using 2.25mm hook and Scheepjes Organicon
Sweet Mandarin (223), make a magic ring.

Round 1: 5 sc into ring. (5 sts)

Round 2: [2 sc in next st] 5 times. (10 sts)

Round 3: [2 sc in next st, 1 sc] 5 times. (15 sts).

Round 4: [2 sc in next st, 2 sc] 5 times. (20 sts)

Rounds 5 to 7: 20 sc.

Round 8: [2 sc in next st, 1 sc] 10 times. (30 sts)

Round 9: 5tr-cl, 18 sc, 5tr-cl, 10 sc. (30 sts)

Rounds 10 to 12: 30 sc.

Round 13: [1 sc, invdec] 10 times. (20 sts)

Insert 4mm safety eyes between Rounds 7 and
8, on either side of the Iguana's head. There are 7
sts between the eyes.

Stuff the head.

(C)– **Round 14:** [invdec, 2 sc] 5 times. (15 sts)

Round 15: 15 sc.

Round 16: [2 sc, 2 sc in next sts] 5 times. (20 sts)

Round 17: [1 sc, 2 sc in next sts] 10 times. (30 sts)

Rounds 18 to 26: 30 sc.

Round 27: [invdec, 4 sc] 5 times. (25 sts)

Switch to Scheepjes Organicon Curly Dock
(225).

Round 28: 25 sc.

(D)– **Round 29:** [invdec, 3 sc] 5 times. (20 sts)

Did you know?

Iguanas are incredibly versatile
reptiles with amazing adaptations!
They can regenerate lost tails, which
helps them escape predators. Many
iguanas have specialised toe pads
that allow them to climb smooth
surfaces effortlessly. Some species
can even change colour to blend into
their surroundings or communicate
with other iguanas. By controlling
insect populations and serving as prey
for larger animals, iguanas play vital
roles in our ecosystems.

Switch to Scheepjes Organicon Sweet Mandarin (223).

Round 30: 20 sc.

Round 31: [invdec, 2 sc] 5 times. (15 sts)

Rounds 32 and 33: 15 sc.

Make sure to stuff before the opening becomes too small. Switch to Scheepjes Organicon Curly Dock (225).

Round 34: 15 sc.

Round 35: [invdec, 1 sc] 5 times. (10 sts)

Switch to Scheepjes Organicon Sweet Mandarin (223).

Rounds 36 and 37: 10 sc

Round 38: [invdec, 3 sc] 2 times. (8 sts)

Round 39: 8 sc.

Switch to Scheepjes Organicon Curly Dock (225).

Round 40: 8 sc.

Round 41: [invdec, 2 sc] 2 times. (6 sts). Mark this round to reconnect the yarn for the dorsal crest later.

Switch to Scheepjes Organicon Sweet Mandarin (223).

Rounds 42 to 45: 6 sc.

Switch to Scheepjes Organicon Curly Dock (225).

Round 46: 6 sc.

Round 47: [invdec, 1 sc] 2 times. (4 sts)

Rounds 48 to 50: 4 sc.

(A) Fasten off, close and weave in ends.

Eyelids

(B) Double over a strand of Scheepjes Organicon Sweet Mandarin (223) and embroider eyelids over the top part of the eyes. Make about 3 to 4 sts.

Legs (make 4)

Using 2.25mm hook and Scheepjes Organicon Sweet Mandarin (223), make a magic ring.

Round 1: 6 sc in ring. (6 sts)

Round 2: [2 sc in next st, 2 sc] 2 times. (8 sts)

Rounds 3 and 4: 8 sc.

Round 5: [invdec, 2 sc] 2 times. (6 sts)

Rounds 6 to 10: 6 sc.

(C) Close, fasten off and leave a long tail to sew onto the Iguana's body. Sew the front legs onto Round 16 on either side of the body and the back legs onto Round 27 on either side of the body.

Dorsal crests

(D)
(E)
Use a piece of contrasting yarn to mark a line all the way up the Iguana's spine. Connect Scheepjes Organicon Curly Dock (225) through a stitch (back to front) on Round 41 of the tail and work your way up the spine.

Row 1: 1 slst, [2 sc, ch 2, skip last st of ch, 1 sc in next st of ch] 7 times, [2 sc, ch 3, skip next 2 sts of ch, 1 sc in ch] 5 times, [2 sc, ch 4, skip last st of ch, 3 sc in ch] 3 times, slst.

Fasten off and weave in ends.

Dewlap

Use a piece of contrasting yarn to mark a line under the Iguana's chin. Connect Scheepjes Organicon Curly Dock (225) through a stitch (back to front) on Round 8.

Row 1: 1 slst, 7 sc. (8 sts). Turn, ch 2 (do not count as sts).

Row 2: 4 dc, 3 hdc, 1 sc. (8 sts). Turn, ch 1.

(F)
Row 3: Skip first st, 1 sc, 3 hdc, 3 dc, slst into next st on Iguana's body.

Fasten off and weave in ends.

Tree Prince & Squirrel

The Tree Prince presides over lush forests, where towering trees create intricate habitats teeming with life. He ensures the vitality and balance of forest ecosystems, from dense jungles to expansive woodlands and serene groves. As the protector of verdant realms, the Tree Prince plays a crucial role in maintaining the health and interconnectedness of terrestrial life.

Forests are vital for biodiversity conservation, serving as habitats for countless plant and animal species. They contribute to climate regulation by absorbing carbon dioxide and releasing oxygen, thereby mitigating the impacts of climate change. Forests also provide essential ecosystem services such as soil stabilization, water purification, and nutrient cycling, benefiting both wildlife and human communities.

The Tree Prince symbolises the resilience and majesty of forests in sustaining life on Earth. By honouring the Tree Prince, we acknowledge the profound importance of forests in maintaining global biodiversity, supporting livelihoods, and fostering a deeper connection with nature. Let us protect and cherish our forests, ensuring they thrive as sanctuaries of life and sources of inspiration for the future.

DIFFICULTY LEVEL: INTERMEDIATE

Tree Prince

Finished size: 20cm (8in)

YARNS

Krea Deluxe Organic Cotton 45, Krea Deluxe Organic Cotton 39, Scheepjes Organicon Aloeswood (241), Scheepjes Organicon Sweet Apple (212), Krea Deluxe Organic Cotton 42, Teddy's Wool Starlight Silver

HOOKS

2mm, 2.25mm

Arms and head

A – Using 2.25mm hook and Scheepjes Organicon Aloeswood (241), create the arms and large head following the general pattern (see Making the basic doll).

Ears (make 2)

Using 2.25mm hook and Scheepjes Organicon Aloeswood (241), make a magic ring.

Round 1: ch 2, 1 dc, 4 sc, p, 1 sc in ring.

Fasten off and leave a long tail. Use the tail to sew the ears on either side of the doll's head, centering them between Rounds 13 and 14, 5 sts away from the eyes.

Then make the legs and lower body following the instructions below.

Boots and legs

Using 2.25mm hook and Krea Deluxe Organic Cotton 45, ch 4.

Round 1: Skip last st of ch, 2 sc in one side of ch, 3 sc into first st of ch, 2 sc in opposite side of ch. (7 sts)

Place marker.

Round 2: 3 sc in first st, 2 sc, 3 sc in next st, 3 sc. (11 sts)

Round 3: 1 sc, [3 sc in next st, 4 sc] 2 times. (15 sts)

Round 4: 1 sc, *[2 sc in next st] 3 times, 4 sc; repeat from * once more. (21 sts)

Trace the sole of the boot on a piece of cardboard, cut it out and save to insert into the boot for more stability. This step is optional.

Round 5: BLO 21 sc.

Rounds 6 and 7: 21 sc.

Round 8: [invdec] 4 times, 13 sc. (17 sts)

Round 9: [invdec] 2 times, 13 sc. (15 sts). Insert the sole into the boot.

Rounds 10 to 16: 15 sc.

Round 17: FLO 1 sc, 1 hdc, [1 dc, p, 1 dc] in next st, 1 hdc, 1 sc, switch to Krea Deluxe Organic Cotton 42, BLO 10 sc.

Round 18: 6 sc in BLO, 10 sc. (16 sts)

B – **Rounds 19 to 34:** 16 sc.

Round 35: 10 sc.

Fasten off and set aside to connect to second leg later. Make the second leg the same through to Round 34 , then work 2 sc to move to joining point.

C – **Round 35:** Ch 2, connect both legs by 16 sc around first leg, 2 sc into ch, 16 sc around second leg, 4 sc into opposite side of ch. (36 sts)

NOTE: Adjust sts if necessary to make sure both feet are facing forward by sc more or fewer sts around the legs in Round 35.

Place marker.

Body

Continue working in the round.

Round 1: [2 sc, 2 sc in next st] 2 times, 22 sc, [2 sc in next st, 2 sc] 2 times, 2 sc. (40 sts)

Rounds 2 to 5: 40 sc.

Round 6: [3 sc, invdec] 8 times. (32 sts)

Round 7: 32 sc.

D – Stuff the tips of the toes, insert your wire frame, continue stuffing the legs.

Switch to Scheepjes Organicon Aloeswood (241).

Round 8: BLO 32 sc.

Round 9: 32 sc.

Continue working on the body following the general large torso and neck instructions (see Making the basic doll).

Hair

Using 2.25mm hook and Scheepjes Organicon Sweet Apple (212), measure about 20cm (8in) of yarn, create hair strands following the general instructions (see Making the basic doll). Make the strands about 6 sts long.

Leaf vest (make 2 leaves)

Using 2.25mm hook and Krea Deluxe Organic Cotton 39, ch 10, slst in first st to form a circle, taking care not to twist your sts.

Round 1: ch 2 (counts as first dc), 19 dc in ring, slst in first st to close. (20 sts)

Round 2: Ch1 (counts as first dc), 1 dc working tog with ch, * ch1, 1 dc in previous st, 1 dc working tog with previous dc; repeat from * 20 times, slst in first st to close (counts as last ch-1 sp).

Round 3: ch 1 (does not count as sc) [3 sc in next ch-1 sp] 2 times, [2 sc, 1 hdc] in next ch-1 sp, [2hdc, 1 dc] in next ch-1 sp, [3 dc in next ch-1 sp] 5 times, [2 dc, 1 trbl] in next ch-1 sp, [1 trbl, 2dc] in next ch-1 sp, [3 dc in next ch-1 sp] 5 times, [1 dc, 2 hdc] in next ch-1 sp, [1 hdc, 2 sc] in next ch-1 sp, [3 sc in next ch-1 sp] 2 times, slst in first st to close.

Round 4: ch 1 (does not count as sc), [1 sc, ch 2, skip next st] 15 times, p, [ch 2, skip next st, 1 sc] 15 times, slst in first st to close.

(E)- Fasten off and weave in ends.

Make a second leaf, don't fasten off.

(F)- Hold both leaves together, right sides facing in. 20 slst through BLO of front leaf and FLO of back leaf.

Switch to Teddy's Wool Starlight Silver.

(G)- **Round 5:** BLO 145 sc around both leaves. Fasten off and weave in ends.

Place the vest on your doll and close it with a piece of yarn.

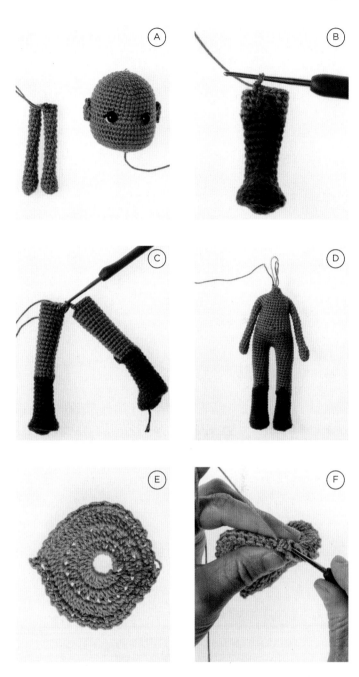

Leaf wings

Small leaf (make 2)

Using 2.25mm hook and Krea Deluxe Organic Cotton 45, ch 20.

(A) **Round 1:** Skip last st of ch, 4 sc, 4 hdc, 5 dc, 5 trbl, 8 trbl in next st (first st of ch), working into opposite side of ch, 5 trbl, 5 dc, 4 hdc, 4 sc.

Round 2: ch 5, skip last st of ch, slst into next 4 sts of ch, continue working into BLO of leaf, 5 sc, 6 hdc, 9 dc, [3 dc in next st] 2 times, p, [3 dc in next st] 2 times, 9 dc, 6 hdc, 5 sc.

Fasten off and weave in ends.

Medium leaf (make 2)

Using 2.25mm hook and Krea Deluxe Organic Cotton 42, ch 25.

Round 1: Skip last st of ch, 6 sc, 6 hdc, 8 dc, 3 trbl, 8 trbl in next st (first st of ch), working into opposite side of ch, 3 trbl, 8 dc, 6 hdc, 6 sc.

(B) **Round 2:** Ch 5, skip last st of ch, slst into next 4 sts of ch, continue working into BLO of leaf, 6 sc, 8 hdc, 11 dc, [3 dc in next st] 2 times, p, [3 dc in next st] 2 times, 11 dc, 8 hdc, 6 sc.

Fasten off and weave in ends.

Place the medium leaf on top of the small leaf, right sides facing in, 23 slst through the BLO of both leaves to connect them.

Large leaf (make 2)

Using 2.25mm hook and Krea Deluxe Organic Cotton 39, ch 30.

Round 1: Skip last st of ch, 8 sc, 10 hdc, 7 dc, 3 trbl, 8 trbl in next st (first sts of ch), working into opposite side of ch, 3 trbl, 7 dc, 10 hdc, 8 sc.

(C) (D) **Round 2:** ch 5, skip last st of ch, slst into next 4 sts of ch, continue working into BLO of leaf, 8 sc, 12 hdc, 10 dc, [3 dc in next st] 2 times, p, [3 dc in next st] 2 times, 10 dc, 12 hdc, 8 sc.

Fasten off and weave in ends.

Place the large leaf on top of the medium leaf, right sides facing together, 26 slst through the BLO of both leaves to connect them.

Fasten off and weave in ends.

(E) Using 2.25mm hook and Teddy's Wool Starlight Silver, slst around BLO of the wing.

(F) Make a second wing the same, taking care to mirror the order of the leaves.

Give the wings a quick iron to make them lie flat.

Mini acorn

Top

Using 2.25mm hook and Scheepjes Organicon Aloeswood (241), make a magic ring.

Round 1: 4 sc in ring. (4 sts)

Round 2: [2 sc in next st] 4 times. (8 sts)

Round 3: 8 sc.

Fasten off and leave a long tail to sew onto the bottom part of the acorn.

Bottom

Using 2mm hook and Scheepjes Organicon Oat Bath (242), make a magic ring.

Round 1: 4 sc in ring. (4 sts)

Round 2: [2 sc in next st] 4 times. (8 sts)

Rounds 3 and 4: 8 sc. Fasten off and weave in ends.

Stuff and sew the top onto the bottom part tightly.

Thread a piece of yarn through all the wings' leaf stems and the little acorn, and then tie around the doll's neck, keeping the acorn to the front.

Crown

Using 2.25mm hook and Teddy's Wool Starlight Silver, ch 42, slst in first st to form a circle, taking care not to twist the sts.

Round 1: Ch 2 (counts as first dc), 41 dc. (42 sts)

Round 2: *Skip next 2 sts, [3 dc, p 3 dc] in next st, skip next 2 sts, 1 slst in next st. Repeat from * 5 more times.

Fasten off and weave in ends. Place the crown on the doll's head.

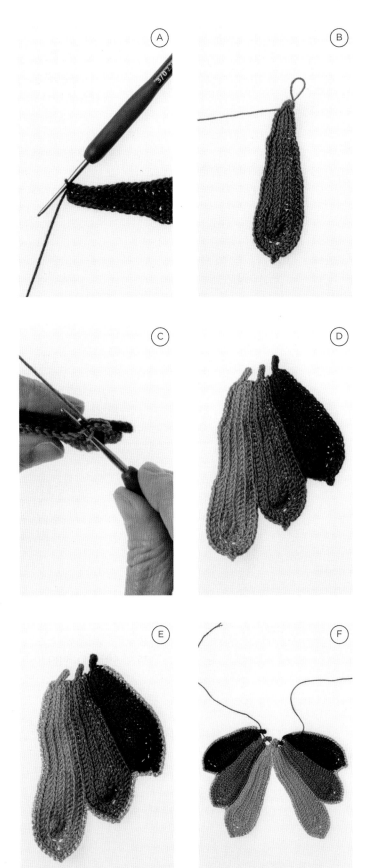

Did you know?

Squirrels are nature's acrobats, capable of jumping up to 10 times their body length! These agile creatures play important roles in forest ecosystems by spreading seeds, which helps plants grow in new areas. They have sharp claws for climbing trees and a keen sense of smell to find buried nuts. Squirrels also communicate with each other through a variety of vocalisations and tail movements, showing their social intelligence.

Little Squirrel Friend

Finished size: 8cm (3⅛in)

YARNS

Scheepjes Organicon Maple Bark (226), Scheepjes Organicon Hickory (240), Scheepjes Organicon Soft Cloud (202)

HOOK

2.25mm

Head

Using 2.25mm hook and Scheepjes Organicon Maple Bark (226), make a magic ring,

Round 1: 6 sc into ring. (6 sts)

Round 2: [2 sc in next st] 6 times. (12 sts)

Round 3: [2 sc in next st, 1 sc] 6 times. (18 sts)

Round 4: [2 sc in next st, 2 sc] 6 times. (24 sts)

Rounds 5 to 7: 24 sc.

Round 8: [2 sc in next st, 1 sc] 12 times. (36 sts)

Rounds 9 to 12: 36 sc.

(A) **Round 13:** [1 sc, invdec] 12 times. (24 sts)

Stuff the head firmly, making sure you stuff the cheeks really well. Insert 4mm safety eyes between Rounds 8 and 9.

Round 14: [invdec] 12 times. (12 sts)

Round 15: [invdec] 6 times. (6 sts)

Close, fasten off, weave in ends and leave a long tail to sew onto the body. Embroider a little nose with black embroidery yarn on Round 10.

Ears (make 2)

Using 2.25mm hook and Scheepjes Organicon Maple Bark (226), ch 8, slst in first st to form a circle, taking care not to twist your sts. Leave a long piece of yarn before creating the chain to sew the ears onto the Squirrel's head later.

Round 1: 8 sc into ch.

Round 2: [invdec, 2 sc] 2 times. (6 sts)

Round 3: [invdec, 1 sc] 2 times. (4 sts)

(B) Close, fasten off and cut the yarn about 6mm (¼in) short and fray it to create a tiny tassel. Sew the ears onto either side of the Squirrel's head between Rounds 13 and 14. There are 6 **sts** between both ears.

Feet and body

Using 2.25mm hook and Scheepjes Organicon Maple Bark (226), ch 3.

Round 1: Skip last st of ch, 1 sc into ch, 3 sc in last sts of ch, 1 sc into opposite side of ch. (5 sts)

Round 2: 3 sc in first st, 1 sc, 3 sc in next st, 2 sc. (9 sts)

Round 3: BLO 9 sc.

Round 4: 9 sc.

Round 5: 1 sc, invdec, 6 sc. (8 sts)

Round 6: 8 sc.

Make another foot the same through to Round 6, then work 2 sc to move to joining point.

(C) Connect the feet:

Round 7: Ch 1, connect by 8 sc around the first foot, 1 sc into ch, 8 sc around the second foot, 1 sc into opposite side of ch. (18 sts)

NOTE: Adjust sts if necessary to make sure both feet are facing forward by sc more or fewer sts around the legs in Round 6.

Place marker.

Continue working in the round for the body.

Round 1: [2 sc in next st] 9 times. (27 sts)

Rounds 2 to 5: 27 sc.

Round 6: Invdec, 23 sc, invdec. (25 sts)

Round 7: [3 sc, invdec] 5 times. (20 sts)

Round 8: 20 sc. Stuff tightly.

Round 9: [2 sc, invdec] 5 times. (15 sts)

Rounds 10 and 11: 15 sc.

Round 12: [1 sc, invdec] 5 times. (10 sts)

(D) **Round 13:** [invdec] 5 times. (5 sts). Close, fasten off and weave in ends.

(E) Sew head onto body.

Tummy patch

Using 2.25mm hook and Scheepjes Organicon Soft Cloud (202), ch 5.

Round 1: Skip last sts of ch, 3 sc, 3 sc in last st, 3 sc in opposite side of ch. (9 sts)

Round 2: 3 sc in first st, 3 sc, 3 sc in next st, 4 sc. (13 sts)

Round 3: 2 sc in next st, 1 sc, 2 sc in next st, 3 sc, 2 sc in next st, 1 sc, 2 sc in next st, 4 sc. (17 sts)

Round 4: 2 sc in next st, 2 sc, 2 sc in next st, 5 sc, 2 sc in next st, 2 sc, 2 sc in next st, 4 sc. (21 sts)

Fasten off and leave a long tail to sew onto the top of the Squirrel's tummy.

Arms (make 2)

Using 2.25mm hook and Scheepjes Organicon Maple Bark (226), make a magic ring.

Round 1: 6 sc in ring. (6 sts)

Round 2: 2 sc in next st, 5 sc. (7 sts)

Round 3: 7 sc.

Round 4: 5 sc, invdec. (6 sts)

Rounds 5 to 8: 6 sc.

Close, fasten off and leave a long tail. Sew onto Round 9 on either side of the body.

Tail

Using Scheepjes Organicon Maple Bark (226) and Scheepjes Organicon Aloeswood (241) together, make 4 mini pompons about 5cm (2in) in circumference. Thread them on top of each other to create the tail. Sew the tail onto the bottom back of the squirrel tightly and trim it down to make it look neat.

(A)

(B)

(C)

(D)

(E)

(F)

(G)

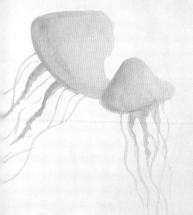

Ocean King & Stingray

The Ocean King reigns over the vast seas with grace and wisdom, embodying the deep love we have for nature. His presence ensures harmony among sea creatures, from the tiniest fish to the largest whales. By maintaining balance in marine ecosystems, he helps the ocean flourish with life and beauty.

Oceans are not just bodies of water; they are the lifeblood of our planet, covering over 70% of Earth's surface and supporting a staggering array of life forms. They regulate climate, provide food and livelihoods for millions of people, and produce oxygen essential for life on Earth. Our oceans also inspire awe and wonder, showcasing the profound beauty and diversity of marine life.

The Ocean King symbolises the immense power and significance of oceans in our world. By honouring him, we honour the essential role of marine ecosystems in ecological balance, biodiversity conservation, and human well-being. Let us protect and cherish our oceans, ensuring they remain vibrant and resilient for generations to come.

DIFFICULTY LEVEL: INTERMEDIATE

Ocean King

Finished size: 30cm (12in)

YARNS

Krea Deluxe Organic Cotton 53, Krea Deluxe Organic Cotton 23, Krea Deluxe Organic Cotton 21, Scheepjes Organicon Deep Sleep 256, Teddy's Wool Starlight Silver

HOOK

2.25mm

(A) Arms and head

Using 2.25mm hook and Krea Deluxe Organic Cotton 53, crochet the arms and large head of your Merman following the general pattern instructions (see Making the basic doll).

Tail and fins

Large fins (make 2)

The fins are worked flat, working back and forth in rows. Turn and ch after each row. All rows are worked into BLO.

Using 2.25mm hook and Krea Deluxe Organic Cotton 21, ch 18.

Row 1: P, 1 sc, 4 dc, 2 hdc, 8 sc. (15 sts + p)

(B) **Row 2:** BLO, turn, ch 1, skip next st, 13 sc.

Row 3: BLO, turn, ch 5 (+ ch 3 for p) p, 2 sc, 4 dc, 2 hdc, 7 sc. (15 sts + p)

Row 4: BLO, turn, ch 1, skip next st, 12 sc.

Row 5: BLO, turn, ch 5 (+ ch 3 for p) p, 2 sc, 4 dc, 2 hdc, 6 sc. (14 sts)

Row 6: BLO, turn, ch 1, skip next st, 11 sc.

Row 7: BLO, turn, ch 5 (+ ch 3 for p), p, 2 sc, 4 dc, 2 hdc, 5 sc. (13 sts)

Row 8: BLO, turn, ch 1, skip next st, 10 sc.

Row 9: BLO, turn, ch 5 (+ ch 3 for p), p, 2 sc, 4 dc, 2 hdc, 4 sc. (12 sts)

Row 10: BLO, turn, ch 1, skip next st, 9 sc.

Row 11: BLO, turn, ch 6 (+ ch 3 for p), p, 2 sc, 5 dc, 2 hdc, 6 sc, 1 sc in ch 1 of Row 10, 3 sc in 3 free sc of Row 9, 1 sc in ch 1 of Row 8, 3 sc in 3 free sc of Row 7, 1 sc in ch 1 of Row 6, 3 sc in 3 free sc of Row 5, 1 sc in ch 1 of Row 4, 3 sc in 3 free sc of Row 3, 1 sc in ch 1 of Row 2, 1 sc in ch 1. (32 sts)

Row 12: BLO, turn, ch 1, skip next st, 26 sc.

(C) **Row 13:** BLO, turn, ch 2 (+ ch 3 for p), p, 2 sc, 5 dc, 2 hdc, 3 sc. (12 sts + p)

Row 14: BLO, turn, ch 1, skip next st, 6 sc.

Row 15: BLO, turn, ch 2 (+ 3 ch for p), p, 2 sc, 4 dc, 2 hdc, continue working into Row 11, [invdec, 1 sc] 2 times. (12 sts)

Rows 16 and 17: Repeat Rows 14 and 15 once.

Row 18: Repeat Row 14 once more.

Row 19: BLO, turn, ch 2 (+ 3 ch for p), p, 2 sc, 4 dc, 2 hdc, continue working into Row 11, invdec, 1 sc, slst to close. (11 sts)

Fasten off and weave in ends.

Make second fin using 2.25mm hook and Krea Deluxe Organic Cotton 23.

Small fins (make 3)

Yarn quantity: 15g

Using 2.25mm hook and Krea Deluxe Organic Cotton 21, ch 18.

Row 1: P, 1 sc, 4 dc, 2 hdc, 8 sc. (15 sts + p)

Row 2: BLO, turn, ch 1, skip next st, 13 sc.

Row 3: BLO, turn, ch 5 (+ ch 3 for p) p, 2 sc, 4 dc, 2 hdc, 7 sc. (15 sts + p)

Row 4: BLO, turn, ch 1, skip next st, 12 sc.

Row 5: BLO, turn, ch 5 (+ ch 3 for p) p, 2 sc, 4 dc, 2 hdc, 6 sc. (14 sts)

Row 6: BLO, turn, ch 1, skip next st, 11 sc.

Row 7: BLO, turn, ch 5 (+ ch 3 for p), p, 2 sc, 4 dc, 2 hdc, 8 sc, 1 sc in ch 1 of Row 6, 3 sc in 3 free sc of Row 4, 1 sc in ch 1 of Row 3, 3 sc in 3 free sc of Row 2, 1 sc in ch 1 of Row 1. (25 sts + p)

Row 8: BLO, turn, ch 1, skip next st, 22 sc.

Row 9: BLO, turn, ch 2 (+ ch 3 for p), p, 2 sc, 5 dc, 2 hdc, 3 sc. (12 sts + p)

Row 10: BLO, turn, ch 1, skip next st, 6 sc.

Row 11: BLO, turn, ch 2 (+ 3 ch for p), p, 2 sc, 4 dc, 2 hdc, continue working into Row 8, [invdec, 1 sc] 2 times. (12 sts)

Rows 12 and 13: Repeat Row 10 and 11 once.

Rows 14: Repeat Row 10 once more.

Row 15: BLO, turn, ch 2 (+ 3 ch for p), p, 2 sc, 4 dc, 2 hdc, slst to close.

Fasten off and weave in ends.

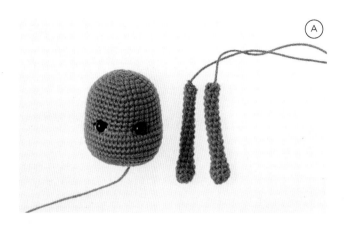

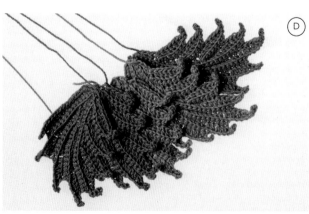

Tail body

Yarn quantity: 20g (¾oz)

(A) Using 2.25mm hook and Krea Deluxe Organic Cotton 21, create a loop on your hook, stack the top ends of 2 large fins and one small fin on top of each other and 3 sc through all 3 fins.

Row 1: Turn, ch 1, [2 sc in next st] 3 times. (6 sts)

Close with slst to form a circle.

Place marker.

Continue working in the round.

(B) **Round 2:** [2 sc in next st] 6 times. (12 sts)

Round 3: [2 sc in next st, 1 sc] 6 times. (18 sts)

Rounds 4 to 6: 18 sc.

Round 7: BLO [2 hdc around front post of next st, 2 hdc] 6 times. (24 sts)

Round 8: BLO 24 sc.

Rounds 9 to 12: 24 sc.

Round 13: BLO [2 hdc in next st, 2 hdc] 8 times. (32 sts)

Round 14: BLO 32 sc.

Rounds 15 to 20: 32 sc.

Round 21: BLO [2 hdc in next st, 7 hdc] 4 times. (36 sts)

Round 22: BLO 36 sc.

(C) **Rounds 23 to 29:** 36 sc.

Round 30: BLO 36 hdc.

Round 31: BLO 36 sc.

Rounds 32 to 38: 36 sc.

Round 39: BLO 36 hdc.

Round 40: BLO 36 sc.

Round 41: [invdec, 7 sc] 4 times. (32 sts)

Rounds 42 to 44: 32 sc.

Attaching the side fins to the tail

(D)
(E) **Round 45:** 6 sc, place the narrow end of one side fin on top of the tail and 3 sc through both to connect them, 12 sc; repeat for the second fin, 8 sc. (32 sts)

You can also sew the side fins onto the tail later if you prefer.

Round 46: BLO 32 sc.

Switch to Krea Deluxe Organic Cotton 53.

Round 47: 32 sc.

Stuff the tip of the tail, insert your wire frame, continue stuffing the tail.

Tail decorations

(F) Using 2.25mm hook and Teddy's Wool Starlight Silver, connect the yarn to the top FLO of all the ridges on the tail and slst all around. Slst into last st to close, fasten off and weave in ends.

(G)
(H) Using 2.25mm hook and Teddy's Wool Starlight Silver, slst around FLO of all fins.

(I) Follow the Large Doll pattern for the torso and neck (see Making the basic doll).

(A) Hair and beard

Yarn quantity: 30g (1oz)

Use 2.25mm hook and Scheepjes Organicon Blue Orchid (252).

Measure 25cm (10in) of yarn and fold it double without cutting it. Follow the instructions for creating hair (see Making the basic doll), making the hair strands between 8 and 10 sts, the moustache strands 5 sts and beard strands between 15 and 20 sts.

Crown

(B)
(C) Trace the crown template (see Templates) with 2mm (14 gauge) wire. Make a small indentation on both ends of the wire to secure the yarn. Wrap Teddy's Wool Starlight Silver tightly around the wire. Tie off the end and shape the finished crown around the doll's head.

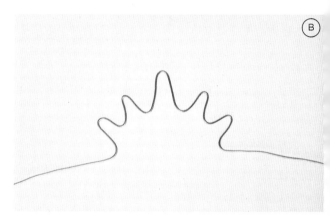

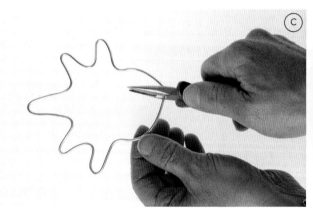

Little Stingray Friend

Finished size: 10cm (4in)

YARNS

Krea Deluxe Organic Cotton 51 Scheepjes Organicon Oxygen 219

HOOK

2.25mm

The Stingray is worked back and forth in rows. Turn and ch after each row (the ch does not count as a st). Keep the increases and decreases loose so they don't distort your work.

Using 2.25mm hook and Krea Deluxe Organic Cotton 51, ch 5.

Row 1: Skip last st of ch, 4 sc into ch. (4 sts). Turn, ch 1.

Row 2: 2 sc in next st, 2 sc, 2 sc in next st. (6 sts). Turn, ch 1.

Row 3: 6 sc. Turn, ch 1.

Row 4: 2 sc in next st, 4 sc, 2 sc in next st. (8 sts). Turn, ch 1.

Row 5: 2 sc in next st, 6 sc, 2 sc in next st. (10 sts). Turn, ch 1.

Row 6: 2 sc in next st, 8 sc, 2 sc in next st. (12 sts). Turn, ch 1.

Row 7: 3 sc in next st, 10 sc, 3 sc in next st. (16 sts). Turn, ch 1.

Row 8: 3 sc in next st, 14 sc, 3 sc in next st. (20 sts). Turn, ch 1.

Row 9: 3 sc in next st, 18 sc, 3 sc in next st. (24 sts). Turn, ch 1.

Row 10: 3 sc in next st, 22 sc, 3 sc in next st. (28 sts). Turn, ch 1.

Row 11: 3 sc in next st, 26 sc, 3 sc in next st. (32 sts). Turn, ch 1.

Row 12: 32 sc. Turn, ch 1.

Row 13: sc3tog, 26 sc, sc3tog. (28 sts). Turn, ch 1.

Row 14: sc3tog, 22 sc, sc3tog. (24 sts). Turn, ch 1.

Row 15: sc2tog, 20 sc, sc2tog. (22 sts). Turn, ch 1.

Row 16: sc2tog, 18 sc, sc2tog. (20 sts). Turn, ch 1.

Row 17: sc2tog, 16 sc, sc2tog. (18 sts). Turn, ch 1.

Row 18: sc2tog, 14 sc, sc2tog. (16 sts). Turn, ch 1.

Row 19: sc2tog, 12 sc, sc2tog. (14 sts). Turn, ch 1.

Row 20: sc2tog, 10 sc, sc2tog. (12 sts). Turn, ch 1.

Row 21: sc2tog, 8 sc, sc2tog. (10 sts). Turn, ch 1.

Row 22: sc2tog, 6 sc, sc2tog. (8 sts). Turn, ch 1.

Row 23: sc2tog, 4 sc, sc2tog. (6 sts). Turn, ch 1.

Row 24: sc2tog, 2 sc, sc2tog. (4 sts). Turn, ch 1.

Did you know?...

Stingrays play key roles in marine ecosystems. As predators, they control populations of smaller animals and by stirring up the seabed they promote nutrient cycling. They also provide food for larger predators. Stingrays have the ability to detect the electrical signals of other animals. This special sense, called electroreception, helps them find prey hidden in the sand.

(A) **Row 25:** [sc2tog] 2 times. (2 sts)

Fasten off and weave in ends.

(B) Using 2.25mm hook and Scheepjes Organicon Oxygen (219), crochet Rows 1 to 25 one more time.

(C) Connecting the halves of the Stingray

Place both halves of the Stingray on top of each other, wrong sides facing each other.

(D) Using 2.25mm hook and 2 strands of Krea Deluxe Organic Cotton 51, make a loop on your hook and sc into the first sts of both halves of the Stingray, continue working through both halves to connect them.

Round 1: 3 hdc in first st, 2 sc, 3 hdc, [12 sc, 3 sc in next st] 2 times, ch 13, skip last st of ch, 12 sc into ch, stuff the center of the Stingray lightly, [3 sc in next st, 12 sc] 2 times.

Fasten off and weave in ends.

(E)
(F) Embroider eyes between Rows 3 and 4 using the bullion st. Add a little smiley mouth over Rows 5 and 6 on the white side of the Stingray.

(G) Use Teddy's Wool Starlight Silver to embroider dots on the gray side using bullion sts.

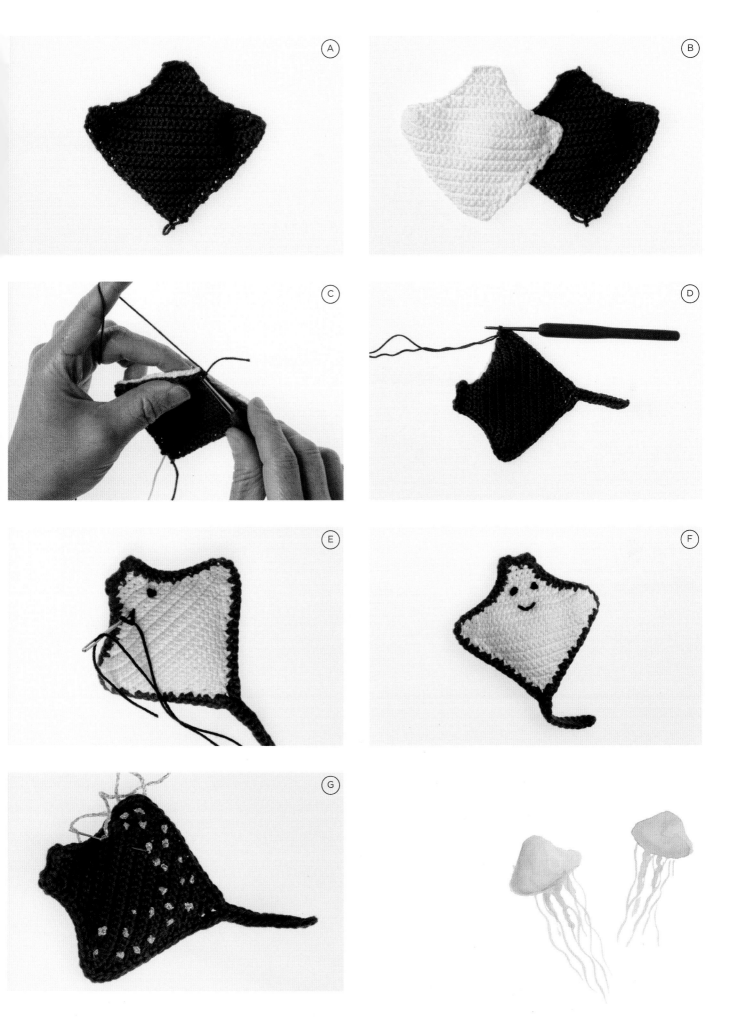

Lady of the Lake & Turtle

The Lady of the Lake reigns over serene waters, where tranquil beauty meets vital biodiversity. She ensures the health and balance of aquatic ecosystems, from shimmering lakes to flowing rivers and peaceful ponds. Lakes are the jewels of our planet, bustling with life and home to playful fish, singing frogs, graceful birds, and lush plants. They provide the fresh water we need every day and help keep our climate balanced, ensuring temperatures stay just right and weather patterns remain healthy. Lakes are critical for nutrient cycling, water filtration, and flood regulation, contributing to the overall health of surrounding landscapes and communities.

As the protector of aquatic serenity, the Lady of the Lake plays a crucial role in preserving the richness and interconnectedness of water-based life.

Let us cherish and protect our lakes, ensuring they remain vibrant sources of life and inspiration for generations to come.

DIFFICULTY LEVEL: EASY TO INTERMEDIATE

Lady of the Lake

Finished size: 20cm (8in)

YARNS

Krea Deluxe Organic Cotton 22, Scheepjes Organicon Oat Bath (242), Scheepjes Organicon Soft Sky (216), Teddy's Wool Starlight Silver

HOOKS

2.25mm, 2.5mm

Arms and head

Using 2.25mm hook and Scheepjes Organicon Oat Bath (242), make the arms and large head using the general pattern instructions (see Making the basic doll).

(A)- Lashes

Embroider 2 small lashes on the outside of the eyes.

Feet and legs

Using 2.25mm hook and Scheepjes Organicon Oat Bath (242), ch 4.

Round 1: Skip last st of ch, 2 sc into one side of ch, 3 sc into first st of ch, 2 sc into opposite side of ch. (7 sts)

Place marker.

Round 2: 3 sc into first st, 2 sc, 3 sc in next st, 3 sc. (11 sts)

Round 3: 11 sc.

Create the heel by working back and forth. Do not ch 1 after turn.

(B)- **Row 4:** 7 sc, turn, sc2tog, 2 sc, sc2tog.

Continue working in the round.

Round 5: Turn, 4 sc, 1 sc into space between heel and top of foot, 6 sc into top of foot, 1 sc into space between top of foot and heel. (12 sts)

Place marker.

Round 6: 4 sc, invdec, 4 sc, invdec. (10 sts)

Rounds 7 to 12: 10 sc.

Round 13: [2 sc in next st, 4 sc] 2 times. (12 sts)

Rounds 14 and 15: 12 sc.

Round 16: 11 sc, 2 sc in next st. (13 sts)

Rounds 17 to 28: 13 sc.

Round 29: 5 sc, stop here.

Fasten off and set aside to attach to second leg later.

Make second leg the same through to Round 28, then work 12 sc to move to joining point.

(C)- **Round 29:** Ch 2, connect by 13 sc around first leg, starting after the fastened-off sts, 2 sc into ch, 13 sc around second leg, 2 sc into opposite side of ch. (30 sts)

Place marker.

Body

Continue working in the round for the body.

Round 1: 2 sc, 2 sc in next st, 1 sc, 2 sc in next st, 19 sc, 2 sc in next st, 1 sc, 2 sc in next st, 3 sc. (34 sts)

Rounds 2 to 6: 34 sc.

Stuff the tips of the toes, insert your wire frame, continue stuffing the legs.

Round 7: 7 sc, invdec, 15 sc, invdec, 8 sc. (32 sts)

(D)-
(E)- Follow the Large Doll pattern for the torso and neck (see Making the basic doll).

(F)- ## Hair

Yarn quantity: 50g (1¾oz)

Use 2.25mm hook and Scheepjes Soft Sky (216).

Measure out about 96cm (38in) and create the hair following the general instructions (see Making the basic doll) making hair strands of 35 to 45 sts.

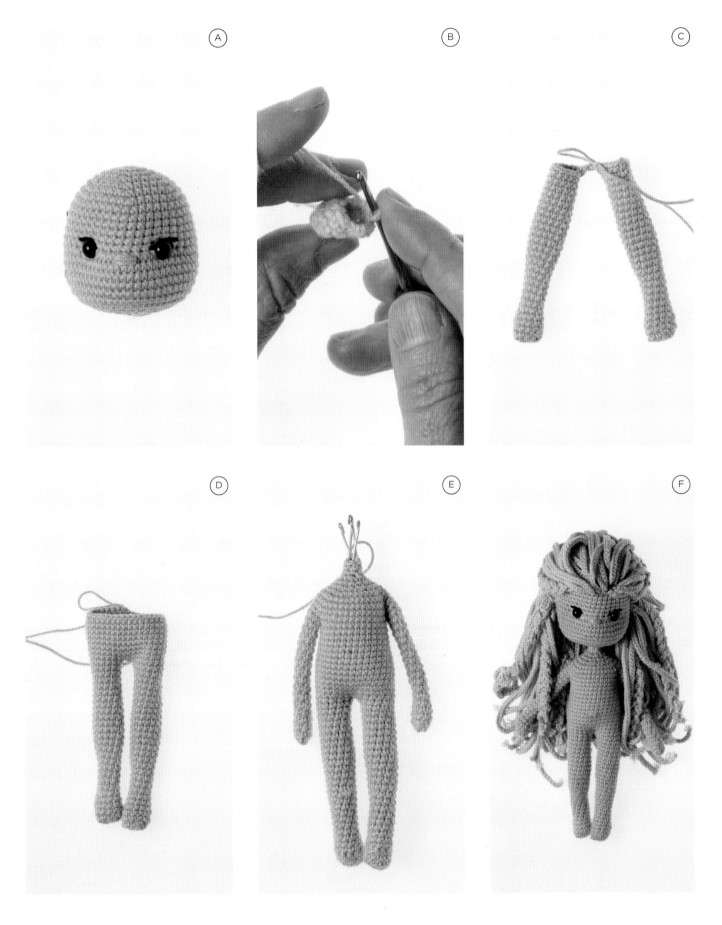

A

B

C

D

E

F

Dress

Yarn quantity: 30g (1oz)

The dress is worked back and forth. Turn and ch at the end of each row (this ch does not count as a st). The entire dress is worked into BLO or FLO.

Using 2.5mm hook and Krea Deluxe Organic Cotton 22, ch 35.

Row 1: Skip last 4 sts of ch, [7 dc, 5 dc in next st] 3 times, 7 dc (43 sts + 4 button hole sts). Turn, ch 1.

(A)- **Row 2:** FLO * 7 sc, [2 sc in next st] 5 times; repeat from * 3 times, 7 sc. (58 sts). Turn, ch 2.

(B)- **Row 3:** BLO 7 dc, skip next 10 sts, 24 dc, skip next 10 sts, 7 dc. (38 sts). Turn, ch 1.

Row 4: FLO 38 sc. Turn, ch 2.

Row 5: BLO 38 dc. Turn, ch 1. Place marker.

Rows 6 to 15: Repeat Rows 4 and 5, 5 times more. Mark Row 15.

Row 16: Repeat Row 4 one more time.

Row 17: BLO [2 dc in next st] 38 times. (76 sts). Turn, ch 1.

Row 18: FLO 76 sc. Turn, ch 2.

(C)- **Row 19:** BLO [2 dc in next st, 1 dc] 38 times. (114 sts). Turn, ch 1.

Row 20: FLO 114 sc. Turn, ch 2.

Row 21: BLO 114 dc. Turn, ch 1.

Rows 22 to 25: Repeat Rows 20 and 21 twice.

Row 26: Repeat Row 20.

Switch to Teddy's Wool Starlight Silver.

Row 27: BLO [3 sc, p] 38 times.

Fasten off and weave in ends.

Sleeves

(D)- Using 2.5mm hook and Krea Deluxe Organic Cotton 22, reconnect the yarn to the bottom st of one sleeve opening, 1 sc, make 2 sc into dc (on the side of sleeve), BLO 11 sc into top of sleeve, make 2 sc in dc (on the other side of sleeve). (16 sts)

Place marker.

(E)- **Round 1:** BLO [2 dc in next st, 1 dc] 8 times. (24 sts)

Round 2: BLO 24 sc.

Round 3: BLO [2 dc in next st, 1 dc] 12 times. (36 sts)

Round 4: BLO 36 sc.

Round 5: BLO [2 dc in next st, 1 dc] 18 times. (54 sts)

Round 6: BLO 54 sc.

Round 7: BLO [2 dc in next st, 1 dc] 27 times. (81 sts)

Round 8: BLO 81 sc.

Round 9: BLO 81 dc.

(F)- **Rounds 10 and 11:** Repeat rounds 8 and 9 once.

Switch to Teddy's Wool Starlight Silver.

Round 12: BLO [3 sc, p] 27 times.

Fasten off.

(G)- ## Dress decorations

Using Teddy's Wool Starlight Silver, connect the yarn to the BLO of neck opening.

(H)- **Row 1:** [3 sc, p] 9 times.

Using Teddy's Wool Starlight Silver, connect the yarn to the front loop of Row 5.

Row 1: [3 sc, p] 12 times.

Using Teddy's Wool Starlight Silver, connect the yarn to the front loop of Row 15.

(I)- **Row 1:** [3 sc, p] 12 times.

Stitch side seams of dress closed.

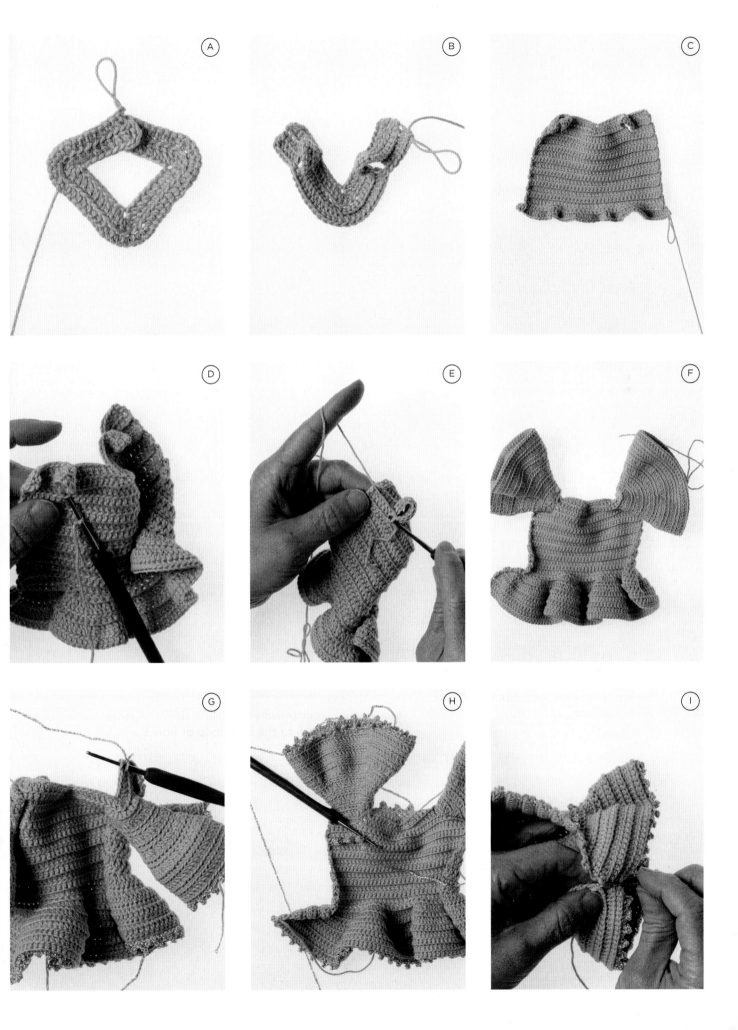

Gathering the sleeves

(A)— Fold the sleeves in half lengthwise, thread a
(B) piece of yarn through the top length of the
sleeve and pull tight to gather. Close tightly,
fasten off and weave in ends.

Water drop

Using hook 2.25mm and Teddy's Wool Starlight
Silver, make a magic ring.

Round 1: 3 sc, p, 1 sc, slst into first sc to close.

Fasten off and leave a long tail to sew onto the
doll's forehead.

Did you know?...

Turtles play vital roles in our
ecosystems. As predators, they
regulate populations of insects
and fish. They also consume
fruits and plants, which aids in
seed dispersal and promotes
plant growth. Their nesting
and burrowing enhances
biodiversity.

Little Turtle Friend

Finished size: 8cm (3⅛in)

YARNS

Krea Deluxe Organic Cotton 42, Krea Deluxe Organic Cotton 39, Scheepjes Organicon Sweet Apple (212)

HOOK

2.25mm

Legs (make 4)

Using 2.25mm hook and Krea Deluxe Organic Cotton 39, make a magic ring.

Round 1: 6 sc into ring. (6 sts)

Round 2: [2 sc in next st] 6 times. (12 sts)

Round 3: [2 sc in next st, 1 sc] 6 times. (18 sts)

Round 4: 18 sc.

Fold the circle in half, stuff lightly, 9 sc through BLO and FLO of both halves of the circle to crochet them together.

Leave the loop to connect to the underside of the Turtle later.

Head

Using 2.25mm hook and Krea Deluxe Organic Cotton 39, make a magic ring.

Round 1: 6 sc into ring. (6 sts)

Round 2: [2 sc in next st] 6 times. (12 sts)

Round 3: [2 sc in next st, 1 sc] 6 times. (18 sts).

Rounds 4 and 5: 18 sc.

Round 6: [2 sc in next st, 1 sc] 9 times. (27 sts)

Rounds 7 to 10: 27 sc.

Round 11: [1 sc, invdec] 9 times. (18 sts)

Insert 4mm safety eyes between Rounds 5 and 6 on either side of the Turtle's head. There are 7 sts between the eyes.

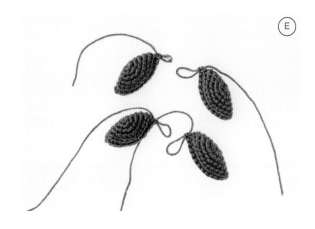

Stuff the head firmly, making sure you stuff the cheeks really well.

Round 12: 18 sc.

Round 13: [1 sc, invdec] 6 times. (12 sts)

Round 14: [1 sc, invdec] 4 times. (8 sts)

Creating the neck

Continue working in the round.

Rounds 15 to 17: 8 sc.

(A) **Round 18:** close the neck horizontally and 4 sc through both sides of sts to close.

Insert a wire into the head to give it more stability. This step is optional.

Fasten off and weave in ends.

Plastron (underbelly)

Using 2.25mm hook and Scheepjes Organicon Sweet Apple (212), make a magic ring.

Round 1: 6 sc into ring. (6 sts)

Round 2: [2 sc in next st] 6 times. (12 sts)

Round 3: [2 sc in next st, 1 sc] 6 times. (18 sts)

Round 4: [2 sc in next st, 2 sc] 6 times. (24 sts)

Round 5: [2 sc in next st, 3 sc] 6 times. (30 sts)

Round 6: [2 sc in next st, 4 sc] 6 times. (36 sts)

Round 7: [2 sc in next st, 5 sc] 6 times. (42 sts)

(B)
(C)
(D)
(E) **Round 8:** *6 sc, insert your hook into the next st, place the loop of one of the legs onto your hook and 1 sc through all loops on hook; repeat from * one more time, 4 sc.

To connect the head, place the neck of the Turtle under the plastron, 4 slst loosely through the plastron and neck to connect them (make sure you hold the head upside down so it will face the correct way when you turn the Turtle over), 5 sc, *insert your hook into the next st, place the loop of one of the legs onto your hook and 1 sc through all loops on your hook, 6 sc; repeat from * one more time, stop the Round.

Fasten off and weave in ends.

If you prefer, you can sew the legs and head onto the plastron at the indicated placements.

Carapace (shell)

Using 2.25mm hook and Krea Deluxe Organic Cotton 42, make a magic ring.

Round 1: 6 sc in ring. (6 sts)

Round 2: [3 hdc in next st] 6 times. (18 sts)

Round 3: BLO 18 sc.

Round 4: [1 sc, 3 hdc in next st, 1 sc] 6 times. (30 sts)

Round 5: BLO 30 sc.

Round 6: [2 sc, 3 sc in next st, 2 sc] 6 times. (42 sts)

Round 7: BLO 42 sc.

Round 8: 42 sc.

Round 9: BLO [3 sc, 1 hdc, 3 sc] 6 times. (42 sts)

(F) **Round 10:** Place the carapace on top of the Turtle's plastron, lining up the points of the carapace and plastron. Slst all around, through the BLO of the carapace and FLO of the body to connect them. Make sure to stuff firmly before you close completely. (42 sts). You can also sew the pieces together, if you prefer.

Round 11: 3 sc, [3 hdc in next st, 6 sc] 6 times, 3 sc. (60 sts)

Fasten off and weave in ends.

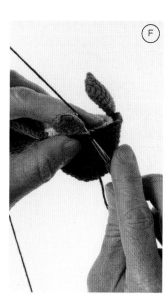

Arctic Prince & Penguin

The Arctic Prince reigns over the icy and pristine landscapes of the polar regions, embodying resilience and beauty in the face of extreme conditions. As the protector of polar wonders, from majestic polar bears to nimble arctic foxes and elusive seals, he plays a crucial role in maintaining the delicate balance of this unique and fragile environment.

As a vital component of Earth's climate system, the Arctic regulates global temperatures and influences weather patterns. Its icy waters are home to a wealth of marine life, including whales and countless fish species. Polar bears, uniquely adapted to the harsh conditions, are apex predators that play a key role in controlling marine mammal populations.

The Arctic Prince symbolises the resilience and adaptability of life in extreme environments, highlighting the importance of preserving these fragile ecosystems in the face of climate change.

By honouring the Arctic Prince, we celebrate the enduring marvels of the polar world and its role in maintaining our planet's health.

DIFFICULTY LEVEL: EASY

Arctic Prince

Finished size: 14.5cm (5¾in)

YARNS

Krea Deluxe Organic Cotton 02, Krea Deluxe Organic Cotton 17, Krea Deluxe Organic Cotton 20, Scheepjes Organicon Oxygen (219), Scheepjes Organicon Frosted Silver (203), Teddy's Wool Starlight Silver

HOOKS

2.25mm, 2.5mm

(A) Arms and head

Using 2.25mm hook and Krea Deluxe Organic Cotton 02, make the arms using the general pattern instructions (see Making the basic doll) and stop after Round 11.

Make the head following the small head instructions (see Making the basic doll).

Feet and legs

Using 2.25mm hook and Krea Deluxe Organic Cotton 02, ch 3.

Round 1: Skip last st of ch, 1 sc into one side of ch, 3 sc into first st of ch, 1 sc into opposite side of ch. (5 sts)

Place marker.

Round 2: 3 sc into first st, 1 sc, 3 sc in next sts, 2 sc. (9 sts)

Round 3: 9 sc.

Create the heel by working back and forth. Do not ch 1 after turn.

Row 4: 5 sc, turn, sc2tog, 1 sc, sc2tog.

Continue working in the round.

(B) Round 5: Turn, 3 sc, 1 sc into space between heel and top of foot, 5 sc into top of foot, 1 sc into space between top of foot and heel. (10 sts)

Place marker.

Round 6: 3 sc, invdec, 3 sc, invdec. (8 sts)

Rounds 7 to 10: 8 sc.

Round 11: [2 sc in next sts, 3 sc] 2 times. (10 sts)

Rounds 12 to 15: 10 sts.

Round 16: 2 sc.

Fasten off and set aside to attach to second leg later. Make second leg the same through to Round 15, then work 8 sc to move to joining point.

(C) Round 16: Ch 2, connect by 10 sc around first leg, starting after the fastened-off st, 2 sc into ch, 10 sc around second leg, 2 sc into opposite side of ch. (24 sts)

NOTE: Adjust sts if necessary to make sure both feet are facing forward by sc more or fewer sts around the legs in Round 16.

Place marker.

Body

Continue working in the round for body.

Round 1: [1 sc, 2 sc in next sts] 2 times, 14 sc, [2 sc in next sts, 1 sc] 2 times, 2 sc. (28 sts)

Rounds 2 and 3: 28 sc.

Stuff the tips of the toes, insert your wire frame and continue stuffing the legs.

Work the torso and neck using the general pattern instructions (see Making the basic doll).

Hair

Yarn quantity: 30g (1oz)

Using 2.25mm hook and Scheepjes Oxygen (219), measure about 25cm (10in) and create the hair following the general instructions (see Making the basic doll) making hair strands of around 7 to 9 sts.

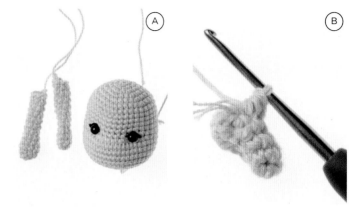

Hooded cape

The cape is worked back and forth in rows. Turn and ch after each row (ch does not count as st).

Hood

Using 2.5mm hook and Teddy's Wool Starlight Silver, ch 64.

Row 1: Skip last st of ch, 63 hdc into ch. (63 sts) Turn, ch 1.

Switch to Krea Deluxe Organic Cotton 20.

Row 2: FLO 63 sc.

Rows 3 to 11: 63 sc. Turn, ch 1.

Row 12: [5 sc, sc2tog] 9 times. (54 sts) Turn, ch 1.

Row 13: 54 sc. Turn, ch 1.

Row 14: [4 sc, sc2tog] 9 times. (45 sts). Turn, ch 1.

Row 15: 45 sc. Turn, ch 1.

Row 16: [3 sc, sc2tog] 9 times. (36 sts). Turn, ch 1.

Row 17: 36 sc.

Row 18: [2 sc, sc2tog] 9 times. (27 sts). Turn, ch 1.

Row 19: [1 sc, sc2tog] 9 times. (18 sts). Turn, ch 1.

Row 20: [sc2tog] 9 times. (9 sts)

Close and fasten off, leave a long tail and sew the edges together until Row 9.

Cape

Hold the back of the hood facing you and reconnect the yarn to the first st of Row 1.

Row 1: pick up and 20 sc into the edge of the hood. (20 sts). Turn, ch 1.

Row 2: [2 sc into next st, 1 sc] 10 times. (30 sts). Turn, ch 1.

Row 3: [2 sc into next st, 2 sc] 10 times. (40 sts). Turn, ch 1.

Row 4: 40 sc. Turn, ch 1.

Row 5: [2 sc into next st, 3 sc] 10 times. (50 sts). Turn, ch 1.

Row 6: 50 sc. Turn, ch 1.

Row 7: 10 sc, ch 5, skip next 5 sts, 20 sc, ch 5, skip next 5 sts, 10 sc. (40 sts + 2 ch 5)

Row 8: 10 sc, 5 sc into ch, 20 sc, 5 sc into ch, 10 sc. (50 sts)

Rows 9 to 14: 50 sc.

Switch to Teddy's Wool Starlight Silver.

Row 15: * 1 slst, skip next st, [1 dc, 1 ch, 1 dc, p, 1 dc, 1 ch, 1 dc] in next st, skip next st, 1 slst, skip next st, 5 sc in next st; repeat from * 5 more times, 1 slst.

Fasten off and weave in ends.

Hood crown

Using 2.5mm hook and Teddy's Wool Starlight Silver, reconnect the yarn to BLO of Row 1 of the hood.

Row 1: * 1 slst, skip next st, [1 dc, 1 ch, 1 dc, p, 1 dc, 1 ch, 1 dc] in next st, skip next st, 1 slst, skip next st, 5 sc in next st; repeat from * 7 more times.

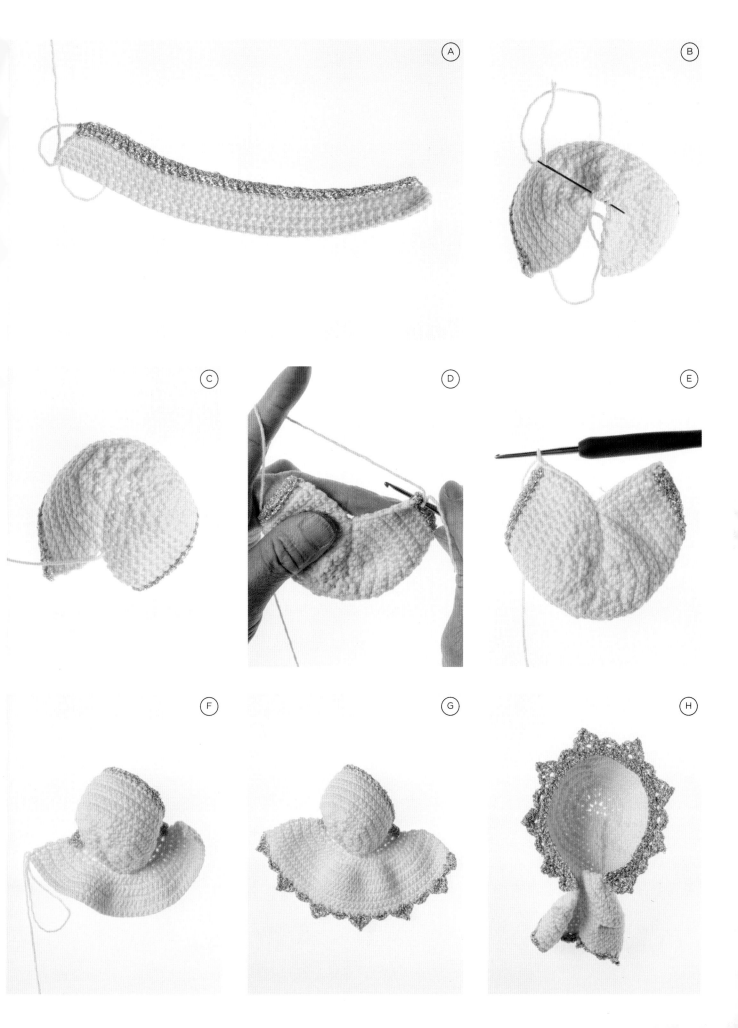

Boots (make 2)

Ⓐ Using 2.25mm hook and Scheepjes Organicon Frosted Silver (203), ch 4.

Round 1: Skip last sts of ch, 2 sc in ch, 3 sc in next st, 2 sc in other side of ch. (7 sts)

Round 2: 3 sc in first st, 2 sc, 3 sc in next st, 3 sc. (11 sts)

Round 3: [2 sc in next st] 3 times, 2 sc, [2 sc in next st] 3 times, 3 sc. (17 sts)

Trace the sole of the boot on a piece of cardboard, cut it out and save to insert into the boot for more stability. This step is optional.

Round 4: BLO 17 sc.

Rounds 5 and 6: 17 sc.

Round 7: 9 sc, [invdec] 3 times, 2 sc. (14 sts)

Insert the cardboard into the boot.

Round 8: 10 sc, [invdec] 2 times. (12 sts)

Rounds 9 and 10: 12 sc.

Switch to Scheepjes Organicon Oxygen (219).

Round 11: 12 reverse sc.

Ⓑ Fasten off and weave in ends.

Dungarees

Using 2.5mm hook and Krea Deluxe Organic Cotton 20, ch 12, slst in first st to form a circle, taking care not to twist your sts.

Round 1: 12 sc in ch. (12 sts)

Place marker.

Round 2: BLO [2 sc in next st] 12 times. (24 sts)

Rounds 3 to 7: 24 sc.

Fasten off and set aside to connect to second trouser leg.

Make second trouser leg the same through to Round 7, don't fasten off.

Ⓒ **Round 8:** Connect both trouser legs by 24 sc around first leg and 24 sc around second leg. (48 sts)

Round 9: [4 sc, invdec] 8 times. (40 sts)

Round 10: [3 sc, invdec] 8 times. (32 sts)

Round 11: [6 sc, invdec] 4 times. (28 sts)

Rounds 12 to 16: 28 sc.

D **Round 17:** [11 hdc, ch 7, skip next 3 sts, hdc in next st] 2 times.

NOTE: You might have to adapt the sts so the armholes (2 skipped sts) are on either side of the dungarees.

Round 18: 11 hdc, 7 hdc around ch, skip next st, 11 sc, 7 hdc around ch, skip next st, 4 sc. (36 sts)

E Fasten off and weave in ends.

Use the chart to embroider the little snowflake onto the front of the dungarees using cross stitch. Each square on the chart corresponds with one crochet stitch.

Snowflake embroidery pattern for dungarees

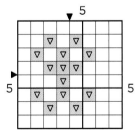

▽ Gray A

Little Penguin Friend

Finished size: 5cm (2in)

YARNS

Krea Deluxe Organic Cotton 28, Krea Deluxe Organic Cotton 48, Scheepjes Organicon Oxygen (219), Scheepjes Organicon Night Shadow (261)

HOOK

2.25mm

Head and body

Using 2.25mm hook and Krea Deluxe Organic Cotton 28, make a magic ring.

Round 1: 6 sc into ring. (6 sts)

Round 2: [2 sc in next st] 6 times. (12 sts)

Round 3: 12 sc.

Round 4: [2 sc in next st, 2 sc] 4 times. (16 sts)

Round 5: 7 sc, [FLO 2dc-cl, ch 2, skip last st of ch, 1 sc in next st of ch, 2dc-cl] in next st, ch 1, 8 sc. (16 sts + 2 clusters)

Ⓐ **Round 6:** 4 sc, 2 sc in next st, 2 sc, BLO 3 sc in next st, 2 sc, 2 sc in next st, 5 sc. (20 sts)

Round 7: 6 sc, switch to Scheepjes Organicon Oxygen (219), (carry the black yarn along the back of your work loosely), 1 sc, 3 dc in next st of round below, 4 sc, 3 dc in next st of round below, 1 sc, switch back to Krea Deluxe Organic Cotton 28, 6 sc. (24 sts)

Switch to Krea Deluxe Organic Cotton 48.

Round 8: BLO 24 sc.

Round 9: 24 sc.

Round 10: 10 sc, [2 sc in next st] 4 times, 10 sc. (28 sts)

Rounds 11 to 16: 28 sc.

Round 17: [5 sc, invdec] 4 times. (24 sts)

Round 18: [4 sc, invdec] 4 times. (20 sts). Stuff tightly.

Round 19: [3 sc, invdec] 4 times. (16 sts)

Round 20: [invdec] 8 times. (8 sts)

Round 21: [invdec] 4 times. (4 sts) Close, fasten off and weave in ends.

Flippers (make 2)

Using 2.25mm hook and Krea Deluxe Organic Cotton 48, make a magic ring.

Round 1: 6 sc into ring. (6 sts)

Round 2: [2 sc in next st, 2 sc] 2 times. (8 sts)

Round 3: 3 sc, 3 sc in next st, 4 sc. (10 sts)

Rounds 4 to 7: 10 sc.

Fasten off and leave a long tail to sew on either side of the Penguin's body between Rounds 7 and 8.

Ⓑ Using a pet brush, brush the whole Penguin until he becomes fluffy.

Feet (make 2)

Using 2.25mm hook and Scheepjes Organicon Night Shadow (261), make a magic ring.

Round 1: 6 sc into ring. (6 sts)

Round 2: [3 sc in next st, 2 sc] 2 times. (10 sts)

Round 3: [3 sc in next st, 4 sc] 2 times. (14 sts)

Rounds 4 and 5: 14 sc.

Pinch the foot closed and work through front and back sts.

Round 6: 2 hdc in next st, 2 slst, 2 dc in next st, *2 slst*, 2 hdc in next st. (10 sts)

Ⓒ Fasten off and weave in ends. Sew the feet next to each other on the bottom of the Penguin.

Ⓐ

Ⓒ

Ⓑ

Did you know?

Penguins are amazing swimmers, using their flippers to "fly" underwater at speeds up to 15 miles per hour! These social birds form large colonies for breeding and protection. Penguins play a crucial role in their ecosystems by controlling fish and krill populations, which maintains a balanced food web. They tolerate life in cold environments by staying warm with thick blubber and dense feathers. Their teamwork in caring for eggs and chicks is truly remarkable.

Night Nymph & Bat

The Night Nymph weaves magic through the shadows, bringing a serene and enchanting beauty to the night. She ensures that nocturnal creatures, from whispering bats to twinkling fireflies, thrive under the starlit sky. As the protector of moonlit mysteries, the Night Nymph plays a crucial role in the nighttime ecosystem, supporting the delicate balance of creatures that come alive after dusk.

Nightlife in nature is vital for many reasons. Nocturnal animals, like bats and owls, control insect populations, pollinate plants, and spread seeds. Predators like foxes and raccoons hunt under the cover of darkness, keeping ecosystems balanced. Even plants rely on the night; many bloom or release fragrances to attract night-flying pollinators. The cool, quiet hours of the night provide a different pace of life, ensuring that every part of the ecosystem has its time and place.

By honouring the Night Nymph, we celebrate the tranquil and mysterious world of the night and the unique beauty it brings to our natural world.

DIFFICULTY LEVEL: INTERMEDIATE TO ADVANCED

Night Nymph

Finished size: 20cm (8in)

YARNS

Krea Deluxe Organic Cotton 11, Krea Deluxe Organic Cotton 48, Krea Deluxe Organic Cotton 20, Scheepjes Night Shadow (261), Scheepjes Organicon Oxygen (219), Scheepjes Organicon Fossil (262), Scheepjes Organicon Ebony (218), Teddy's Wool Starlight Silver

HOOKS

2.25mm, 2.5mm

Arms and head

(A) – Using 2.25mm hook and Krea Deluxe Organic Cotton 11 make the arms and large head using the general pattern instructions (see Making the basic doll).

(B) – Ears (make 2)

Using 2.25mm hook and Krea Deluxe Organic Cotton 11, make a magic ring.

Round 1: ch 2 [1 dc, 3 sc, 1 dc, p, 1 dc, 1 hdc, 1 sc] into ring.

Fasten off and leave a long tail. Sew the ears on either side of the doll's head, centering them between Rounds 13 and 14, 5 sts away from the eyes.

Lashes

Embroider 2 small lashes on the outside of the eyes.

Then make the legs and lower body.

Feet and legs

Using 2.25mm hook and Krea Deluxe Organic Cotton 11, ch 3.

Round 1: Skip last st of ch, 1 sc into one side of ch, 3 sc into first st of ch, 1 sc into opposite side of ch. (5 sts)

Place marker.

Round 2: 3 sc into first st, 1 sc, 3 sc in next st, 2 sc. (9 sts)

Round 3: 9 sc.

Create the heel by working back and forth. Do not ch 1 after turn.

Row 4: 5 sc, turn, sc2tog, 1 sc, sc2tog.

Continue working in the round.

Round 5: Turn, 3 sc, 1 sc into space between heel and top of foot, 5 sc into top of foot, 1 sc into space between top of foot and heel. (10 sts)

Place marker.

Round 6: [3 sc, invdec] 2 times. (8 sts)

Rounds 7 to 9: 8 sc.

Round 10: [2 sc in next st, 3 sc] 2 times. (10 sts)

Rounds 11 to 15: 10 sc.

Round 16: [2 sc in next st, 4 sc] 2 times. (12 sts)

Rounds 17 to 28: 12 sc.

Round 29: 6 sc. Stop round here.

Fasten off and set aside to attach to second leg later. Make second leg the same through to Round 28.

(C) – **Round 29:** Ch 2, connect by 12 sc around first leg, starting after the fastened-off st, 2 sc into ch, 12 sc around second leg, 2 sc into opposite side of ch. (28 sts)

NOTE: Adjust sts if necessary to make sure both feet are facing forward by sc more or fewer sts around the legs in Round 29.

Place marker.

(D) – ## Body

Continue working in the round for body.

Round 1: [1 sc, 2 sc in next st] 2 times, 18 sc, [2 sc in next st, 1 sc] 2 times, 2 sc. (32 sts)

Rounds 2 to 6: 32 sc.

Stuff the tips of the toes, insert your wire frame and continue stuffing the legs.

Follow the general pattern instructions for the torso (see Making the basic doll).

Hair

Yarn quantity: 1¾oz (50g)

Use 2.25mm hook and Scheepjes Ebony (218).

Measure out about 105cm (41in) and create the hair following the general instructions (see Making the basic doll) making hair strands around 50 sts long.

Outfit

Top

The top of the dress is worked back and forth. Turn and ch at the end of each row (ch does not count as a st).

Using 2.5mm hook and Scheepjes Organicon Oxygen (219), ch 34.

Row 1: Skip last st of ch, [10 sc, 2 sc into next st] 3 times. (36 sts). Turn, ch 1.

Row 2: FLO [5 sc, 2 sc in next st] 6 times. (42 sts). Turn, ch 1.

Ⓔ **Row 3:** 6 sc, 2 sc in next st, ch 2, skip 7 sts, 2 sc in next st, 5 sc, [2 sc in next st] 2 times, 5 sc, 2 sc in next st, ch 2, skip 7 sts, 2 sc in first st, 6 sc. (34 sts + 2 ch 2). Turn, ch 1.

Row 4: 8 sc, 2 sc in ch sp, 18 sc, 2 sc in ch sp, 8 sc. (38 sts). Turn, ch 1.

Row 5: 38 sc.

Ⓕ Fasten off and weave in ends. Place onto the doll and close in the back.

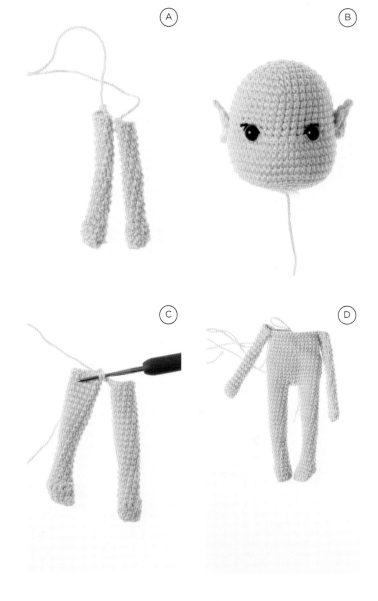

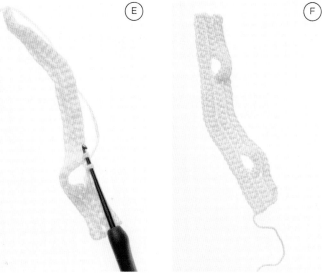

Underskirt

Using 2.5mm hook and Scheepjes Organicon Oxygen (219), ch 32, slst in first st to form a circle, taking care not to twist your sts.

Round 1: 32 sc into ch. (32 sts)

Round 2: BLO *[2 hdc in next st] 7 times, 3 hdc in next st; repeat from * 4 times. (68 sts)

(A) **Round 3:** 15 hdc, 3 hdc in next st, [16 hdc, 3 hdc in next st] 3 times, 1 hdc. (76 sts)

Round 4: 16 hdc, 3 hdc in next st, [18 hdc, 3 hdc in next st] 3 times, 2 hdc. (84 sts)

Round 5: 17 hdc, 3 hdc in next st, [20 hdc, 3 hdc in next st] 3 times, 3 hdc. (92 sts)

Round 6: 18 hdc, 3 hdc in next st, [22 hdc, 3 hdc in next st] 3 times, 4 hdc. (100 sts)

Round 7: 19 hdc, 3 hdc in next st, [24 hdc, 3 hdc in next st] 3 times, 5 hdc. (108 sts)

Round 8: 20 hdc, 3 hdc in next st, [26 hdc, 3 hdc in next st] 3 times, 6 hdc. (116 sts)

Switch to Teddy's Wool Starlight Silver.

(B)
(C) **Round 9:** BLO 21 sc, [1 sc, 1 dc, 2 ch, 1 dc] in next st, *28 sc, [1 sc, 1 dc, 2 ch, 1 dc] in next st; repeat from * 3 times, 7 sc.

Fasten off and weave in ends.

(D) ## Topskirt

(E)
(F) Using 2.5mm hook and Scheepjes Organicon Fossil (262), connect the yarn to the FLO of the 4th st on Round 2 of the underskirt.

Repeat Rounds 2 to 9 of the underskirt.

Thread a thin ribbon or piece of yarn through the sts on Round 1 of the underskirt, place the skirt on your doll and tie in the back.

(G) ## Large Stars (make 4)

Using 2.25mm hook and Teddy's Wool Starlight Silver make a magic ring.

Round 1: [1 sc, 1 hdc, p, 1 hdc] 5 times.

Fasten off and leave a long tail to sew to point of skirt.

Small Stars (make 4)

Using 2.25mm hook and Teddy's Wool Starlight Silver make a magic ring.

Round 1: [1 sc, p] 5 times.

(H) Fasten off and leave a long tail to sew onto each point of the skirt.

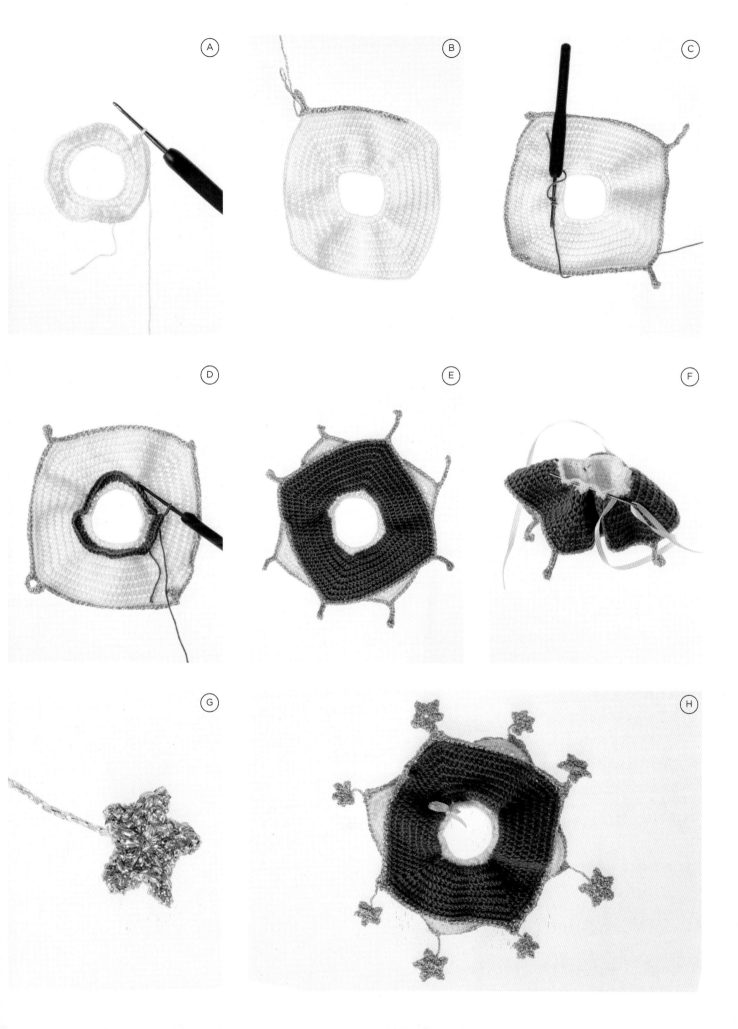

Wings (make 2)

The wings are worked in the round forming a flat circle. Slst and ch after each round, ch counts as first st. After finishing, the circle will be folded in half to form the wings.

Using 2.25mm hook and Scheepjes Organicon Ebony (218), ch 8, slst in first st to form a circle, taking care not to twist your sts.

Round 1: Working around circle: ch 2 (counts as first dc), 2 dc, ch 3, [3 dc, ch 3] 7 times, slst into 3rd dc.

Round 2: Working into ch-3 sps of previous round: ch 2 (counts as first dc), [2 dc, ch 3, 3 dc] in ch-3 sp of previous round, *ch 2, [3 dc, ch 3, 3 dc] in ch-3 sp of previous round; repeat from * 7 times, ch 2, slst into 3rd dc.

Switch to Scheepjes Organicon Night Shadow (261).

Round 3: Working into ch sps of previous round: ch 2 (counts as first dc), 6 dc into ch-3 sp of previous round, ch 2, 1 dc in ch-2 sp of previous round, ch 2, [7 dc into ch-3 sp of previous round, ch 2, 1 dc into ch-2 sp of previous round, ch 2] 7 times, slst into first dc.

Round 4: Ch 2 (counts as first dc), [ch 1, 1 dc] 6 times, *ch 2, skip ch-2 sp, 1 dc (in dc), ch 2, skip ch-2 sp, [1 dc, ch 1] 6 times, dc 1 ; repeat from * 7 times, ch 2, skip ch-2 sp, 1 dc (in dc), ch 2, skip ch-2 sp, slst into first dc.

(A)- It's ok if your circle looks a little wonky at this point, it will straighten out when you fold it in half.

Switch to Krea Deluxe Organic Cotton 48.

Round 5: Ch 2 (counts as first dc in first ch sp), ch 2, [1 dc in ch sp of previous round, ch 2] 63 times, slst into first dc.

Round 6: Ch 2 (counts as first dc), 3 dc in first ch sp of previous round, [4 dc in ch-2 sp of previous round] 4 times, * skip next ch-2 sp, 1 sc into next ch-2 sp, skip next ch-2 sp, [4 dc in next ch-2 sp] 5 times; repeat from * 7 times, skip next ch-2 sp, 1 sc into next ch-2 sp, skip next ch-2 sp, slst into first dc.

Round 7: Ch 2 (counts as first dc), 19 dc, 1 sc, [20 dc, 1 sc] 7 times, slst into 3rd dc.

(A)

(B)

Round 8: Ch 2 (counts as first dc), ch 1, [1 dc, ch 1] 15 times, * skip next 2 dc, 1 sc, ch 1, skip next 2 dc, [1 dc, ch 1] 16 times; repeat from * 7 times, skip next 2 dc, 1 sc, ch 1, slst into first dc.

Round 9: (Ch 2 instead of first dc) *[3 dc in next ch sp, ch 1, skip next ch sp] 8 times, skip next ch sp, 1 sc in sc of previous round, ch 1, skip next ch sp; repeat from * 8 times, slst into third dc.

Switch to Scheepjes Organicon Oxygen (219).

Round 10: (ch 2 instead of first dc) *[6 dc in next ch sp] 7 times, skip next 3 dc + ch, 1 sc (in sc of previous Round), skip next ch + 3 dc; repeat from * 8 times, slst into first dc.

Round 11: (ch 1 instead of first sc) [42 sc, 1 slst] 8 times. (344 sts)

Switch to Teddy's Wool Starlight Silver.

(B) **Round 12:** 344 reverse crochet. Or 344 sc if you prefer.

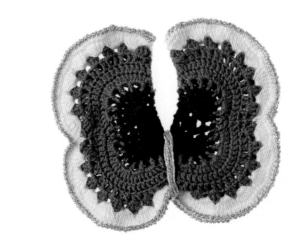

(C) Now is when the magic happens. Fold the circle in half, aligning the points, and wrap Teddy's Wool Starlight Silver yarn around the middle a few times, securing it well (don't pull too tightly). You have just made a beautiful pair of wings! Sew them onto the shoulders of the doll's top.

(D) Butterfly

Large: Crochet Rows 1 to 3 of the wing pattern (you can change the colours to your liking). Fold the circle in half, wrap Teddy's Wool Starlight Silver around the middle of the butterfly and fasten off. Leave a long tail to sew onto the crown.

Small: Crochet Rows 1 and 2 of the wing pattern and continue as for the large butterfly.

(E) Crown

Cut about 18cm (7in) of 0.5mm (24 gauge) wire, shape it around the doll's head and ears and curl the end into a loose spiral (see Templates). Using Teddy's Wool Starlight Silver, wrap yarn around the wire, tightly securing the ends with a knot. Crochet a few stars and butterflies and sew them onto the crown. Place the crown on top of the doll's head.

Little Bat Friend

Finished size: 6.5cm (2½in)

YARN

Scheepjes Organicon Night Shadow (261)

HOOK

2.25mm

Head

Using 2.25mm hook and Scheepjes Organicon Night Shadow (261), make a magic ring.

Round 1: 6 sc into ring. (6 sts)

Round 2: 6 sc.

Round 3: [2 sc in next st] 3 times, 3 sc. (9 sts)

Round 4: [2 sc in next st] 4 times, 5 sc. (13 sts)

Round 5: [2 sc in next st] 8 times, 5 sc. (21 sts)

Rounds 6 to 10: 21 sc.

(A) **Round 11:** [5 sc, invdec] 3 times. (18 sts). Stuff the head firmly.

Round 12: 18 sc.

Round 13: [1 sc, invdec] 6 times. (12 sts)

Round 14: [invdec] 6 times. (6 sts)

Close and fasten off. Using black yarn, embroider an eye on either side of the Bat's head over 2 sts on Round 5. Also embroider a little black nose, making a few sts over the top of Round 1.

Ears (make 2)

The ears are worked back and forth in rows. Turn and ch 1 after each row (ch does not count as st). Using 2.25mm hook and Scheepjes Organicon Night Shadow (261), make a magic circle, ch 1.

Row 1: 1 sc in circle. (1 st). Turn, ch 1.

Row 2: 3 sc in next st. (3 sts). Turn, ch 1.

Row 3: 2 sc in next st, 1 sc, 2 sc in next st. (5 sts). Turn, ch 1.

Row 4: 5 sc. Turn, ch 1.

Row 5: 2 sc in next st, 3 sc, 2 sc in next st. (7 sts). Turn, ch 1.

Row 6: 7 sc. Turn, ch 1.

Row 7: 2 sc in next st, 5 sc, 2 sc in next st. (9 sts). Turn, ch 1.

Row 8: 9 sc. Turn, ch 1.

Row 9: 2 sc in next st, 7 sc, 2 sc in next st. (11 sts)

Fasten off and leave a long tail.

(B) Pinch the bottom of the ear closed and sew onto the side of the Bat's head between Rows 7 and 11. Apply some pink blush on the inside of the ear.

Did you know?

Bats are incredible creatures that use echolocation to navigate in the dark! They emit high-pitched squeaks or chirps and listen for the echoes bouncing off objects. This allows them to locate prey and avoid obstacles while flying at night. Bats play crucial roles in ecosystems by controlling insect populations and pollinating flowers. With over 1,400 species worldwide, bats are diverse and fascinating mammals essential for maintaining healthy environments.

Body

Using 2.25mm hook and Scheepjes Organicon Night Shadow (261), make a magic circle.

Round 1: 6 sc into ring. (6 sts)

Round 2: [2 sc in next st] 6 times. (12 sts)

Round 3: [2 sc in next st, 1 sc] 6 times. (18 sts)

Round 4: [2 sc in next st, 2 sc] 6 times. (24 sts)

Rounds 5 to 8: 24 sc.

Round 9: [invdec] 6 times, 12 sc. (18 sts)

Rounds 10 and 11: 18 sc. Stuff firmly.

Round 12: [invdec, 1 sc] 6 times. (12 sts)

Round 13: [invdec] 6 times. (6 sts)

Close, fasten off and leave a long tail. Sew the head onto the body tightly.

Wings (make 2)

Using 2.25mm hook and Scheepjes Organicon Night Shadow (261), make a magic ring.

Round 1: 6 sc into ring. (6 sts)

Round 2: [2 sc in next st] 6 times. (12 sts)

Round 3: [2 sc in next st, 1 sc] 6 times. (18 sts)

Round 4: [2 sc in next st, 2 sc] 6 times. (24 sts)

Round 5: [2 sc in next st, 3 sc] 6 times. (30 sts)

Round 6: [2 sc in next st, 4 sc] 6 times. (36 sts)

Round 7: [2 sc in next st, 5 sc] 6 times. (42 sts)

Round 8: [2 sc in next st, 6 sc] 6 times. (48 sts)

(C)
(D) Fold the wing double and crochet through BLO of both halves to connect them.

Round 9: BLO [p, 6 sc] 4 times, p. (24 sts)

Fasten off and leave a long tail. Sew onto the back of the head on the bottom of Round 13.

General techniques

Slip knot (or loop)

(A) Wrap your yarn around your crochet hook very loosely to form a loop. Pull the bottom yarn through the loop with your hook and pull closed. You have now created the first stitch of your new project.

Chain (ch)

(B) After creating a slip knot, wrap the yarn from back to front over your hook and draw through the loop, pull to close but not too tight. You have now created your first chain stitch. Make as many stitches as indicated in the pattern.

Slip stitch (slst)

(C) Insert your hook into the stitch as instructed on your work, wrap the yarn over your hook and pull through both the stitch and the loop on your hook.

Magic ring

(D)(E)(F) This is the preferred method to start any amigurumi project or crochet pattern in the round. Start by forming a circle with your yarn, insert hook into circle, wrap your yarn over the hook and draw a loop through, but don't pull the circle tight. Now make a chain by wrapping your yarn over your hook and pulling it loosely through the loop on your hook. Next, make the required number of stitches as given in pattern, starting each stitch by inserting your hook through the beginning circle. When all your stitches are complete, you can pull the yarn tail to close the ring.

Single crochet (sc)

(G)(H)(I) This is the stitch we will use most in this book. Insert your hook into the next stitch (this may be a chain stitch or a stitch from a previous round), wrap your yarn over your hook and pull up a loop, there are two loops on your hook now. Wrap the yarn over your hook once more and pull it through both loops. This is one single crochet stitch. Insert your hook into the next stitch to continue.

Half double crochet (hdc)

(J) Wrap the yarn over your hook before inserting it into the next stitch. Wrap the yarn over your hook again and pull through the stitch, you now have 3 loops on your hook. Wrap the yarn over your hook and pull through all 3 loops.

Double crochet (dc)

(K)(L)(M) Wrap the yarn over your hook before inserting it into the next stitch. Wrap the yarn over your hook again and pull through the stitch, you now have 3 loops on your hook. Wrap the yarn over your hook and pull through 2 of the loops, you now have 2 loops on your hook. Wrap the yarn over your hook again and pull through both loops.

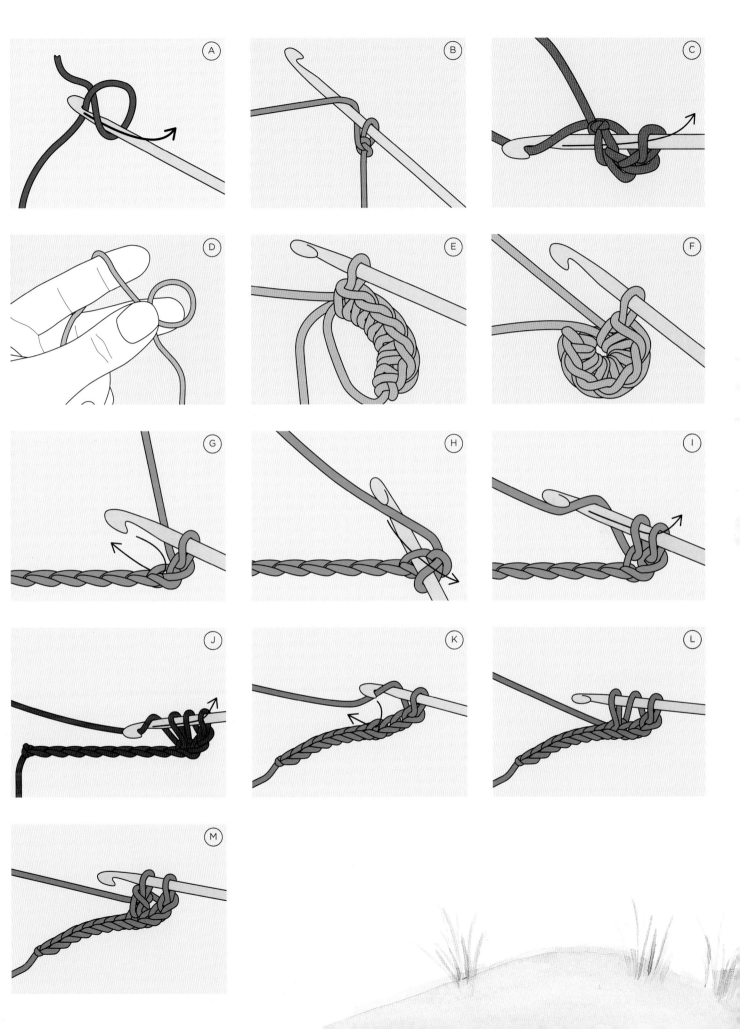

(A) (B) Treble (trbl)

Wrap the yarn over your hook twice before inserting it into the next stitch. Wrap the yarn over your hook again and pull through the stitch. Wrap the yarn over your hook and pull through the first two loops, you now have 3 loops on your hook. Yarn over your hook and pull through the first two loops on the hook again, you now have 2 loops on your hook. Yarn over again and pull through both loops.

(C) Back loop only (BLO)

Insert your hook only into the **back** loop of the next stitch.

(D) Front loop only (FLO)

Insert your hook only into the **front** loop of the next stitch.

(E) (F) (G) Reverse sc (crab stitch)

Insert your hook into the **previous** stitch on your work from front to back and work a single crochet as usual.

(H) (I) (J) Invisible decrease with sc and hdc (invdec)

This decreasing method is my preferred one, it will give you an almost invisible, very neat decrease. Insert your hook into the **front loops** of the next 2 stitches, wrap the yarn over your hook and pull through both front loops, wrap the yarn over your hook again and pull through both loops.

Do the same for hdc invisible decrease – just wrap the yarn over your hook before you insert it into the 2 front loops.

(K) Decrease 1 (or sc2tog)

Insert your hook into the next stitch, yarn over hook and pull up a loop, now insert your hook into the next stitch, yarn over hook and pull up another loop. You now have 3 loops on your hook. Wrap the yarn over your hook and pull through all 3 loops.

(L) (M) Picot (p)

Ch 3, skip last 2 sts of ch, slst into next st.

(N) (O) Cluster stitches (dc-cl and tr-cl)

Work the first stitch of the cluster as normal up to the last pull through, then repeat in the same stitch for the number of stitches stated in the pattern. Wrap the yarn over your hook and pull through all the loops on the hook.

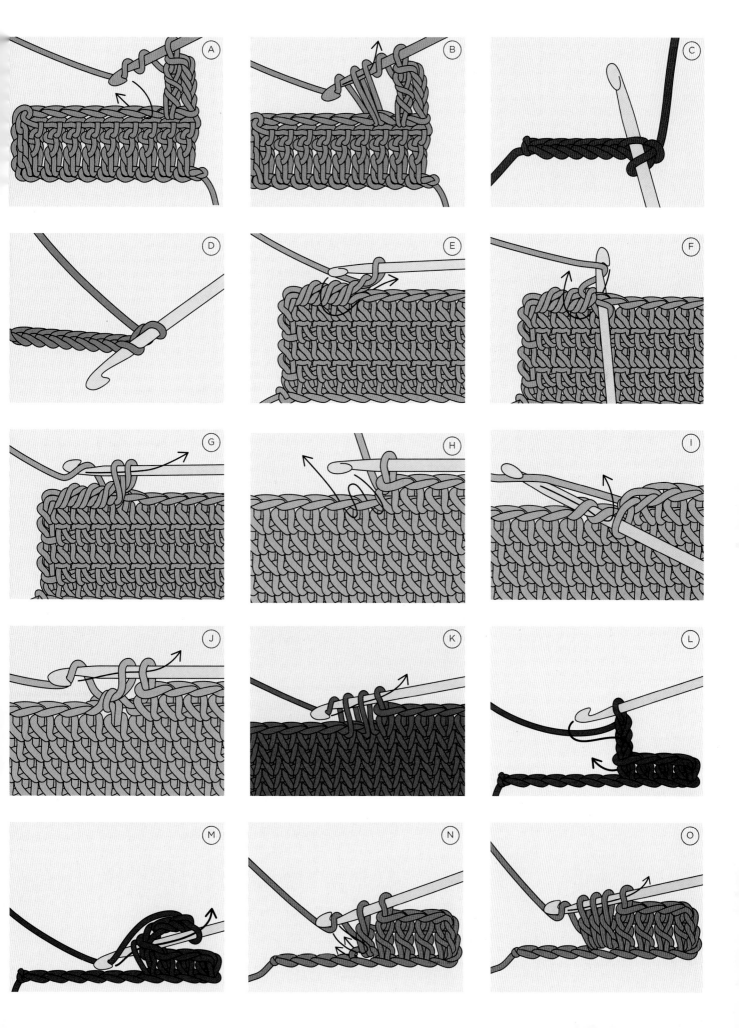

Assembly

(A) Weaving in ends

Thread the yarn onto your tapestry needle, pull the needle through 4–5 sts in one direction, rotate the needle and thread through 4–5 sts in the opposite direction.

(B) Single crochet seam

Insert your hook through both pieces of your work from front to back. Hold your yarn at the back of your work, yarn over and pull up a loop through both pieces. There are now 2 loops on your hook. Yarn over and pull through both loops on your hook. Continue this way to close up the seam.

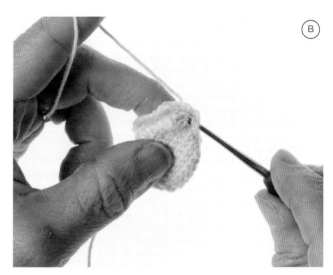

(C) Sewing joins

Thread a piece of yarn onto your tapestry needle (or use the yarn tail from your piece) and use a whip stitch to close the gap or to securely attach your crochet pieces together.

Finishing

(D) (E) Attaching toy safety eyes

Place the toy safety eye into the correct position and secure it by closing it with the flat side of the washer on the inside of your crochet piece. Make sure that you place the eyes correctly because once a washer is fixed in place it is impossible to remove.

(D)

(F) Sewing on buttons

Choose your buttons and thread the needle. Make a little knot at the bottom of the thread. Place the button in the correct place on your crochet work. From the back, push the needle through the holes on your button a few times, then twist the yarn around the base of the button and tie off your yarn.

(E)

(F)

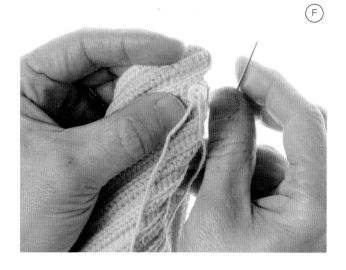

Embroidery stitches

(A) Bullion stitch

Insert the needle through your work from front to back to front again. Wrap the yarn around the tip of the needle a few times, the hold the wraps in place and gently pull the yarn through.This will create a small knot on the top of your work.

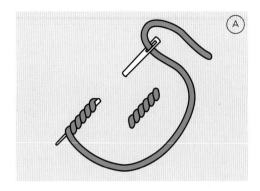

(B) Cross stitch

The single crochet stitch creates a perfect surface for cross stitch. Each stitch represents one square of the grid. Starting from the back of the work, bring your needle through the bottom left corner of your first square. Then work the first diagonal line by bringing it back down through the top right corner of the same square. If you are working a line of cross stitches in the same colour, work this diagonal for all to begin with, starting with the leftmost stitch. Then, work the second diagonal line of the cross by bringing your needle up through the bottom right corner of each square and bridging it back down through the top left corner. Continue for all stitches in that row, working from right to left.

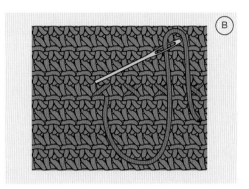

Suppliers

I used the following suppliers for the projects featured in this book:

Scheepjes (yarn): www.scheepjes.com

Krea Deluxe (yarn): www.kreadeluxe.com

ChikaiMakers (safety eyes): www.etsy.com/uk/shop/ChikaiMakers

Tulip (crochet hooks): www.tulip-japan.co.jp

About me

Hi, I'm Nathalie Amiel, the author of *Crochet You!* My journey with yarn began when my great aunt taught me how to knit and crochet as a little girl. Since then, it's grown into something I love sharing with others.

When my sixth child was about one year old, I opened my online crochet and pattern shop. It all started with requests from loving parents, grandparents, and friends who wanted unique, handmade dolls they couldn't find anywhere else. Over the past 10 years, I've created thousands of special dolls that have travelled around the globe, bringing smiles and warm hugs to their new homes.

I'm excited to continue sharing my love for crochet with you and hope to inspire you to create something truly magical. In this book I use crochet to focus on one of my main passions, appreciating and caring for the natural world, and I am pleased to have passed those values onto my daughters. My 11-year-old daughter, Avya, even wrote a poem that I think conveys this message beautifully:

Why don't we save?
Don't put the animals in their grave.

Don't kill the lion for his fur –
he's cute, that's for sure.

Turtles eat and choke on plastic straws –
please stop it, just press pause.

Save the squirrel and the deer –
don't put traps, let's make it clear.

Don't remind me of the circus –
erasing these animals from the surface.

We will all do our small part
and that will be our start!

Templates

These are the templates for the doll wire frames, Night Nymph crown, Tree Prince wire rim glasses, and Ocean King crown. You can trace these full-size templates with wire and then just follow the instructions as stated in the patterns. You can also download printable versions of these templates from: www.bookmarkedhub.com.

Ocean King crown

Insect Lord Glasses

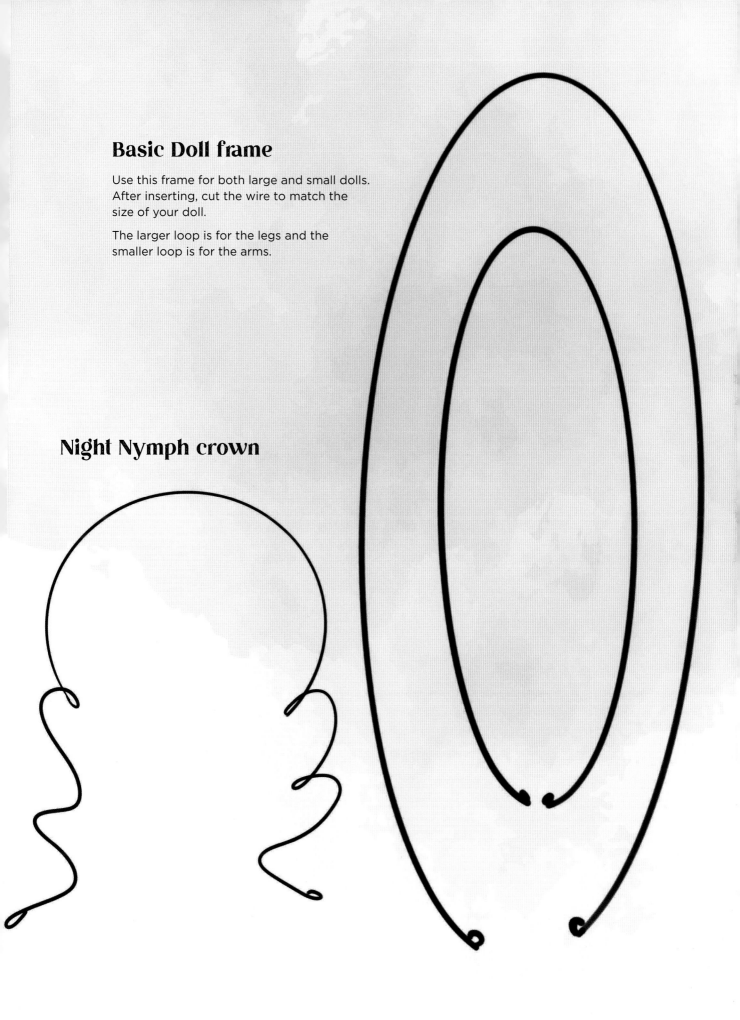

Basic Doll frame

Use this frame for both large and small dolls. After inserting, cut the wire to match the size of your doll.

The larger loop is for the legs and the smaller loop is for the arms.

Night Nymph crown

Thanks

Creating this book has been an incredible journey, and I am deeply grateful to the many wonderful people who have supported me along the way.

First and foremost, I owe an immense debt of gratitude to Sarah Callard. Her unwavering support and guidance have been instrumental in bringing this project to life. A heartfelt thank you goes to the fantastic team at David and Charles – Ame, Jeni, Jessica, Sam, Clare, Jess, Susan, Jason and Beverley. Your professionalism and enthusiasm have made this entire process a delight.

Sincere thanks also to my pattern testers and followers – you are the heart of this creative journey. Your encouragement and feedback have been an endless source of motivation.

A special thank you to Ardon Bar-Hama, who has been my technical lifeline. Your guidance and help in creating the perfect mini studio has allowed me to capture the dolls in their finest light.

To Scheepjes Yarns and Krea Deluxe, I cannot express enough gratitude. Your belief in this project from the very first stitch to the last has been truly inspiring. Your organic yarns are a dream to work with and have added such incredible beauty to this project.

To my family, your love and support have been the foundation of this book. My parents, siblings, and my amazing children. David, for being there since the very first day; Racheli and her husband Yagel, and their little bundles of joy; Matania, for always making me laugh; Aderet, for her steadfast support; and Avya, for her keen eye and playful spirit.

And an extra-special thank you to Orya, whose help was nothing short of amazing throughout this entire process.

Lastly, to my husband Didier, thank you for your endless patience, problem-solving skills, and for always being my biggest cheerleader. Your pride in my work means the world to me.

Making a difference

SINASRA is a non-profit voluntary organization where all funds are exclusively used to assist persons with albinism.

In Africa, living with albinism can be a death sentence. Adults, teenagers, but especially children and infants, can fall victim to brutal attacks and are at serious risk of contracting skin cancer. People with oculocutaneous albinism have little or no pigment in their hair, skin and eyes; thus they are visually impaired and very sensitive to the damaging effects of the sun.

SINASRA's primary concern is the survival of people with albinism, ensuring their livelihood and offering them a fair standard of living. The supply of protective clothing, sunscreen and dissemination of relevant information is aimed at preventing sun-related cancer, its complications and early death. I will donate money for every book I sell to SINASRA. By supporting SINASRA together, we will provide children who suffer from albinism with life saving skin tests, telescopic spectacles and dedicated care that enhances their possibility to live a safe and independent life.

www.sinasra.com

Photo credit: Patricia Willocq

Index

A DAVID AND CHARLES BOOK
© David and Charles, Ltd 2025

David and Charles is an imprint of David and Charles, Ltd, Suite A, Tourism House, Pynes Hill, Exeter, EX2 5WS

Text and Designs © Nathalie Amiel 2025
Layout and Photography © David and Charles, Ltd 2025

First published in the UK and USA in 2025

Nathalie Amiel has asserted her right to be identified as author of this work in accordance with the Copyright, Designs and Patents Act, 1988.

A catalogue record for this book is available from the British Library.

ISBN-13: 9781446314326 paperback
ISBN-13: 9781446314333 EPUB

This book has been printed on paper from approved suppliers and made from pulp from sustainable sources.

Printed in China through Asia Pacific Offset for: David and Charles, Ltd, Suite A, Tourism House, Pynes Hill, Exeter, EX2 5WS

10 9 8 7 6 5 4 3 2 1

Publishing Director: Ame Verso
Senior Commissioning Editor: Sarah Callard
Publishing Manager: Jeni Chown
Editor: Jessica Cropper
Tech Editor: Sam Winkler
Project Editor: Clare Hunt
Design and Art Direction: Jess Pearson
Pre-press Designer: Susan Reansbury
Illustrations: Nathalie Amiel
Photography: Nathalie Amiel and Jason Jenkins
Production Manager: Beverley Richardson

Full-size printable versions of the templates are available to download free from www.bookmarkedhub.com. Search for this book by the title or ISBN: the files can be found under 'Book Extras'. Membership of the Bookmarked online community is free.

David and Charles publishes high-quality books on a wide range of subjects. For more information visit www.davidandcharles.com.

Share your makes with us on social media using #dandcbooks and follow us on Facebook and Instagram by searching for @dandcbooks.

Layout of the digital edition of this book may vary depending on reader hardware and display settings.